You good, Sis?

You good, Sis?

How to turn your pain
into power through
resilience and inner healing.

Monet Cullins

TUCKER
PUBLISHING HOUSE LLC

Paperback ISBN: 978-1-7377140-3-3
Library of Congress Number: 2021917317

Published 2021 by
Tucker Publishing House, LLC
26056 Van Dyke Ave #3502
Centerline, MI 48015
www.tuckerpublishinghouse.com
Published in the United States of America

Dedication

This book is dedicated to the woman who has survived everything that life has thrown at her. The woman who continues to fight her way through no matter how hard it gets.

To the sister who is currently in a domestic violence relationship and is afraid to leave: *You good, Sis?* How is your mental health doing? How are you taking care of yourself? I know it's hard, and you may not know what to do but always remember your mental health comes first. You come first, before your husband, your children, and definitely before any job or business you have. You can't give to them if you are empty. Being in an abusive relationship is draining and exhausting. Make sure you prioritize some time and get with someone to create a safety plan to leave.

This book was written for the broken, hurt, and abused little girl living on the inside of us all. I'm sorry you had to experience the pain of those moments in your childhood. I'm sorry you weren't valued or appreciated; that you were neglected or abused. You didn't deserve that, but you can let go now. You can push forward. It's time to heal, forgive yourself, and move on.

Say this to your traumatized inner child, and let's get started.

> *"Thank you for protecting us. I know those things hurt, and we are angry, but I got it from here. Let's allow the healed woman to rise up. We are choosing to love ourselves and embrace the totality of who we are. It's time to tell the representative version of yourself to retire so we can show up as the best version of ourselves daily."*

To my four beautiful daughters Camille, Cayleigh, Chloe, & Aundrea, thank you for your support during the process of writing this book. You are my inspiration and motivation to keep going.

This book is for you, *Sis, you Good?*

Trigger Warning

This book will include discussion topics such as domestic violence, child abuse, incest, and suicide. I acknowledge that this content may be difficult to process. I also encourage you to care for your safety and emotional well-being during this time. Be sure to take as many moments as you need and complete the mental health check In at the end of each chapter to help channel the emotions that may be triggered.

Table of Contents

Foreword

You good, Sis? This question can be translated in many different ways, and it's all about your tone. The tone of this phrase can be a question or a statement, and it's a phrase that is shared across the world as a different experience.

You good, Sis? It is something that I shared as both a question and a statement to your writer. Having walked through life with her for over a decade, I am closely familiar with the ups, downs, and waves of Monet's life. As one of her best friends, sisters, and confidants, I have experienced and quite frankly ridden the abruptness of emotional rollercoasters that led to the brokenness and breakthrough you will encounter in this book.

Monet intentionally makes you her family in this read; you will experience the rollercoaster of her life that led to the strong mother, CEO, boss, and leader. I would love to tell you that becoming a leader comes with no loss. The reality is that would not be the case. The torment of the rollercoaster and the bumps and bruises that happen along the way brings us to the power and strength of who we are. Though the road may be bumpy or hurtful, do not worry. There's always an end to every rollercoaster.

Let me say it this way: Monet will walk you through your ups and downs, and no matter what you may be going through, she will make sure you are good. I want to take this final moment to tell you. You good, Sis! If you are going through depression, everything is going to be okay. You can overcome this. You good, Sis! If you are going through unhealthy relationships that cause you to be codependent. You good, Sis! If you have dealt with toxic relationships, impulsivity, and anxiety. In that case, you are good because you have picked up this book. Your writer is dedicated to being transparent and making sure that you know you are not alone and that you are not done growing or evolving. You good, Sis!

You are not alone. You are good, Sis; you are not isolated. You good, Sis; You are not broken, and you will get through this. Everything you need to know that says you are good, you just picked it up.

Don't forget it gets a little bumpy but always remember your writer is committed to making sure you know whether it is a statement or a question. You good, Sis.

Without further ado, I give to you your writer, my friend, and sister Monet Cullins.

Cora Jakes-Coleman

Introduction

Within these pages, you will find pieces of me; some parts you may know, some you may not. The truths of my heart are poured into these pages, hoping to change the lives of every single person reading this book. I have begun to embrace vulnerability and transparency as strengths instead of my weaknesses. They are now my superpowers, and I choose to walk in them boldly every day. They are a part of who I am, and I love it! My prayer is that this side of me would penetrate the hearts of women who can not only relate to my story but feel empowered to know they are not alone. We are on a journey to recognize our traumas, get into therapy, heal, and break the next generation's generational curses.

I am a mother to four beautiful daughters, Camille, Cayleigh, Chloe, and Aundrea. They are my entire world; I am the oldest of six daughters from my mother, and I have six nieces and three nephews. I think God has made it very clear that women are my ministry. Apparently, my womb is only meant to carry women so far. When I think about how powerful we are as women, we bring life into this world, and we are the nurturers of the world. We give so much to so many people and rarely take care of ourselves. We must prioritize our self-care daily. I pray this encourages you to do so every day!

The title, "*You good, Sis?*" derives from going through child abuse, domestic violence, and even a suicide attempt. It was hard going through those traumatic experiences and feeling like nobody cared. I felt like I had to suffer in silence. I couldn't talk about what I was going through as a child or an adult, and I felt alone. So, every time someone asked me, "Are you ok?" It helped me understand that people cared about me genuinely and were really concerned about how I was doing. Sometimes when people asked me, "How are you?" I wanted to burst into tears because I couldn't say what I was really feeling.

You good, Sis introduces the idea of checking on your other sisters and asking them, "Are you okay? Is there anything I can do to help you? Can I support you in any way?" Be aware of the people around you. Are they all of a sudden isolated? We must learn to love our neighbor, and that means getting to know them. We must stop turning a blind eye to abuse, neglect, and childhood trauma. Also, having that inward check to ask yourself, is my cup empty? Do I have the capacity to give to anybody else? If not, then what do I need? Do I need to take a break? Or what are some things that I can do to refill my cup so I give it to my children, my business, family, and most importantly myself? So many of us suffer in silence for many different reasons, but we can end that, one woman at a time.

You good, Sis invites you to be a friend to yourself, to be vulnerable and transparent about what you are feeling, to extend yourself grace when things may not go as planned. It's time to love on the hurt little girl inside of you, embrace who you are today, and live your life on purpose!

It's amazing how God will use what we think is the most unattractive thing about ourselves and make it the most beautiful thing we end up loving about ourselves!! I love me and everything about me! Sometimes we allow what people say to affect how we move, what we do and don't do.

Growing up, I always thought my lips were too big for my face, and when I smiled, my eyes were too slanted, so I didn't really like my smile. When I looked in the mirror, I didn't like what I saw. I didn't understand my worth or the destiny God had placed inside me and how He shaped me for where I am today! My mind was clouded with negativity, judgmental thoughts, and lies of other people I took on as my own. I decided to practice doing a mental health check-in with myself daily. I wanted to make sure I was good but also be intentional about checking in with myself.

I began hosting a Clubhouse room called "*You Good, Sis? Mental Health Check-In.*" My room created a safe space for women to be vulnerable, share their experiences. They were empowered by licensed therapists, mental health experts, and a room full of women ready to motivate each other. Sometimes it was hard for me to show up consistently, but it helps to remind me to check in with myself first before I show up for my community.

My coach asked me a question, and it made me pause and reflect before answering the question. "Why don't you trust yourself to do the hard things?" Pausing, I replied, " I do." and quickly changed my answer after realizing I couldn't trust myself because I didn't know who I was. I never chose myself, got to know myself, learned my likes and dislikes, or just loved on myself as a friend to myself. I didn't even know what that looked like or that it was possible. I am so grateful to be on this journey. Yes, it has its challenges, but I learn so much about myself in the process, and *that* reward is worth it. I am worth it. I choose to embrace all that I am and who I am becoming. I'm so honored when other women are inspired by my story. It empowers me to continue to show up for the women God has given me to minister to.

Today I am not the woman I was before. Often, I hear, "Girl, you've changed." And I know it to be true. I look in the mirror now, and I am like, *who is this woman?* God has really transformed my life, and it's amazing to see and feel my growth. I'm honored to be used by God this way.

Initially, I couldn't accept that good things were happening for me. Others would see the change in me and compliment me on my growth, but I didn't see the same things they saw. I didn't believe good things could happen to me because of the mistakes in the past. I had to shift my mindset to fully walk in my purpose.

Proverbs 23:7 says, "For as he thinketh in his heart, so he is." We have the power to "think" ourselves, happy or depressed. Our mind is a very powerful tool, especially when we use it to its full capacity.

In summary, we have the power to control our daily thoughts and, ultimately our minds. As you read this book, open your mind to hear my heart and shift your perspective about mental health and the importance of it. Mental Health and the church go hand in hand, and we must embrace both to truly understand how to deal with it.

Monet Cullens

Chapter 1

The Essence of Me

〰⟨◎〇⟩〰

I magine being 19 sitting in a cold clinic alone, waiting to hear your name called by one of the nurses. I stared at the walls and read the posters over and over again, trying to avoid sitting in the moment. *Am I about to be a mother?* I was so nervous and anxious to find out; my hands were sweaty as I signed the intake documents.

The nurse came to the door, called my name smiling,

and said, "How are you?" I nodded, gave a fake smile, and said, "I'm fine." I slowly walked to the back, with my heart racing, not knowing what was about to happen next. She asked me a few questions about my medical history and explained that the doctor would talk to me after getting the results. She administered the blood and urine test.

A few moments later, the doctor came in and said, "Miss. Cullins, you are about eight weeks pregnant." I froze. I thought, *wow, I have disappointed my dad again. How am I going to tell my mother? What do I say to my granny and great granny?* (who I lived with at the time)

She said, "Based on your last cycle, It seems you will be due around September 26—" before she could finish saying it, she added, "Oh wow! That's your birthday." I was already shaking my head in disbelief.

Even in my shock, I had a sense of humor about the situation. God, you are funny! Due on my Birthday? Wow.

Oh, my goodness, I cannot believe I'm about to be a mother. I immediately started to think about how unprepared I was. I thought about what I had not conquered; the "inner demons" of my past that I had not dealt with. How would they affect my unborn child? I wanted to be a "perfect" mother for my child.

I thought of what everyone would think of me and how I had disappointed my family. I was supposed to be the one to break this generational curse off our bloodline. I wanted to learn a lot more and unlearn even more toxic behaviors before bringing a child into the world.

I have seven sisters and one brother in total between both of my parents. I am the oldest child and oldest grandchild. Taking care of babies and younger siblings became second nature. At an early age, I learned how to babysit, cook and keep the house clean. I remember taking *Home Economics* in high school and bringing a programmed "baby" home for a week, but this is real. I had a hard time accepting this reality. I fell into a deep depression and sadness, but I didn't allow that to stop me! I was still going to classes and working. It was hard, but I managed to push through.

Becoming a mother has always been the greatest joy of my life. I never understood the responsibility and the courage it takes to be a young single mother until I became one. I gained strengths I didn't know I had. Although I enjoyed the feeling of being pregnant and carrying a child, my pregnancy was not an easy one.

I was hospitalized for the first time in Dallas when I was five months pregnant with Camille. The doctor explained early on in my pregnancy that I was extremely high-risk. I needed to be careful with my daily activities to avoid going on bed rest. I immediately felt the weight of the world on my shoulders. It was such a great responsibility to make sure she didn't come early. I felt like I was wearing a sign on my belly that said, "Fragile, handle with care." I started eating healthier, except when I had the cravings, of course. I walked around the campus at my school for extra exercise. I was so excited!

During this time, I had moved back home to Houston with my family for support. So, I commuted back to Dallas to go to my last doctor's appointment before changing to a Houston doctor. I went to my next doctor's appointment, expecting to go back home afterward. When I arrived, I was spotting heavier than usual, and my doctor put me on bed rest. I was stuck there until

I could commute back home or deliver Camille. So, I stayed with my friend at her apartment for a month.

Here I was, a 19-year-old pregnant freshman in college with no support from her father or his family. I was now stuck in another city, unable to travel, and had to figure it out. I had the help and support of my granny, who took me to my doctors' appointments and helped me as much as she could. She handled the entire situation with grace and ease. Although it wasn't an ideal situation, she made sure I had the resources and support I needed. I was stressed and nervous about doing this alone. Camille's father and I were still communicating, but he refused to take responsibility and help me. This was really heavy for me, but I refused to risk my babies' health by going into labor at six months. Things seemed to be getting worse. I depended on many people and often felt helpless about my situation. I couldn't believe I had done this.

One Sunday evening after church, I sat in the living room of our apartment, listening to worship music, rubbing my belly, and praying over Camille. I did this every single day. One thing I learned from my family is that we pray in good and bad times. My great granny reminded me every time she saw me to pray over my womb. This particular time I remember wondering how my mom felt when she was pregnant with me. Did my mom struggle this way emotionally when she was pregnant with me? Did she feel alone? As an adult, I often reflect on my childhood and wonder how certain events affect my life now.

MY CONCEPTION AND UPBRINGING

On September 26, 1987, God blessed this world and my amazing, loving parents with a beautiful baby girl and named her DeShandra Monet! Related by blood but not in their hearts, my parents are half-brother and sister sharing the same father. Yes, you read that right. I am the gift born in incest.

I was born into the insecurities of my parents, feeling their genuine love and excitement for me, and the rejection and embarrassment attached with incest. My identity was shaped and molded to fit those titles. Who knew the identity I carried since being in my mother's womb would affect my relationships and friendships throughout my childhood and into my adult life? I remember randomly wondering why I always wanted to fit in. Why was I so codependent in this friendship or that relationship, while very independent and strong-willed in other areas of my life? I wondered why I always needed validation from people that didn't serve me.

They didn't know it at the time, but my parents bathed me in love, wrapped me in shame, and unintentionally taught me what guilt and rejection looked like. I don't think people recognize the magnitude of how our childhood experiences affect our adult life forever (without forgiveness and word-based inner healing, that is).

When I was about four or five, I remember always feeling confused about something; I couldn't figure it out, but it was as if something was missing, and I just felt a void. I remember being with my dad, mom, and other family members but still feeling empty in a small piece of me.

I will never forget, at age six, being told the truth about who my dad actually was. I remember the day like it was yesterday. My first-grade teacher called me to her desk and said, "DeShandra, get your backpack; your mom is on the way to pick you up." I became excited immediately because what kid doesn't want to go home early? It was a perfect surprise! Or so I thought.

I grabbed my light pink backpack and ran down the long hallways in my elementary school to the office. I could see my mommy through the glass doors standing there with her back turned, signing the paperwork for my sister and me to leave. I pushed the office door open with excitement, ran to her, and gave her the biggest hug ever!

"Hey, mommy! Why are we going home right now?"

Smiling and nodding, she answered, "You'll see when we get there."

We waited for my sister to come down to the office then we headed to my grandparent's house.

"Mommy, we didn't get lunch yet," my sister said.

"Okay, baby. You can eat when we get to your Grandy and Pawpaw's house."

During the car ride there, I felt nervous, excited, and a little scared all at the same time. I had an uneasy feeling, and it wasn't a good one. I didn't know what to expect, so I did what I always did; I studied my mother, her reactions, facial expressions, and even her tone when she spoke. We pulled up to the driveway; she paused and said, "We're going to have a family talk with both of you and uncle Bubba. Ok?" We both nodded and said, "Yes, ma'am." She seemed uneasy and unsure of how this would go.

Sitting in my grandmother's sewing room, staring at sky blue painted walls, I was nervous about what was about to happen. My mommy and uncle Bubba came into the room and closed the door behind them. I felt my identity change within a matter of minutes through a few life-altering words.

In summary, my mommy said, "Your uncle Bubba...is your father."

As my younger sister and I looked at each other with much confusion on our faces and millions of questions in our heads, I asked, "So do we have to call you daddy now?"

"Only if you want to. You can call me whatever you want."

"Okay," I replied, but I was never able to utter the words "Daddy" without feeling uncomfortable or confused.

I remember walking out of the room feeling like my head was spinning. I didn't know what to do with that information. But there it is. There's the missing piece. This is the reason why I have felt this void in my few short years of life, or so I thought. For years, I wondered, Lord, why would you choose ME to be born into this type of situation? Not in an ungrateful way but genuinely interested in the *why*? What am I supposed to do with this information? Who is supposed to be healed or touched by my story? How can we stop this from happening to the next generation?

GENERATIONAL CURSES

The enemy used the innocence of my parents to reintroduce the same generational curse that worked in a previous generation in my family. A generational curse is believed to be passed down from one generation to another due to rebellion against God. If your family line is marked by divorce, incest, poverty, anger, or other ungodly patterns, you're likely operating under a generational curse. We inherit many traits and preferences from our parents that aren't always a positive influence on ourselves or others. Our families have the greatest impact on our development, including the development of our patterns of sin.

You see, the enemy will use whatever attack he thinks may work. He is not creative; he doesn't try "new" ways to tempt us, especially if it worked in the previous generation. Generational curses are real, so is our God, and through him, they can be broken. God instructs us on how to dismantle the attacks and plans of the enemy and how to break the generational curses off our bloodlines. Now, common sense tells us that behavior and attitude problems can run in families, just like physical characteristics of height, weight, hair color, and complexion.

In the same way, certain types of sin can pass from generation to generation. This is particularly true of addictive behaviors such as alcoholism. Similarly, physical and sexual abuse might become ingrained in the psychological legacy of certain families.

However, none of this should be viewed in terms of an irreversible "curse." Spiritual deliverance is available to everyone who sincerely calls upon the name of the Lord. (Romans 10:13)

We have to start by obeying the word of God. When we study and are obedient to God's word, we are more equipped to handle the temptations we face. The key to dismantling the enemy's plans is exposing what the problem or stronghold is. We cannot conquer what we don't know exists. We have to talk about generational curses with our families. Let's stop hiding things under the rug, thinking they will never be exposed, leaving even more people hurt. We get so wrapped up in what people think and how it will be perceived through the eyes of those who weren't directly affected most of the time.

We hold a person's testimony hostage with our secrets. What the enemy meant for evil, God will use for HIS glory. You never know what the next person may be dealing with, even in your family, because we "protect" people that should be exposed and get the help that they need.

The Bible says, "We OVERCOME by the word of our testimony," so why don't we give the people involved an opportunity to share their testimony? I know we all remember the saying, "What goes on in this house stays in this house." It has been dredged in our brains for decades. We keep everything bottled inside. We suffer in silence, and in turn, we hurt people who don't deserve to be hurt. Hurt people hurt people. Healed people heal people. Can you start with your generation? Will you break generational curses of your blood, Sis?

Most people don't understand the power and effects of being born in incest. The conversation is not often the starter piece at Thanksgiving dinner or family gatherings, although this is how our earth began to populate. It happened in the Bible all the time. These situations are not discussed and sometimes covered up because of the embarrassment and guilt that it brings. But when we do that, it only hurts the people involved. Some people don't find out things until they are grown, affecting them their entire life. I can't imagine how painful that would be for someone to go through. Sis, if that's you, I'm sorry, and I pray you get the healing you need and deserve.

Often, the truth hurts, and it's hard to relive the trauma and maybe even scary, but we must be selfless in this act and think about how it could affect everyone involved. I am so grateful to have found out about my parents. I am proud of my parents for having the hard yet necessary conversation with my sister and me. Imagine this happening in a Pastor's family where certain church members and people around you are judgmental, scrutinizing your every move. I can't speak to the specifics of what happened or didn't happen because I wasn't born yet. I can only imagine how hard this must've been for my family to process and "handle correctly."

We could all speculate and say what should or shouldn't happen. We don't know what we would've done at that moment. I can only speak from my perspective and what I experienced. This felt like the elephant in the room for me at family gatherings, and it was what everybody knew but did not talk about.

Shhh, act like it hasn't happened... We don't want to feel the pain or embarrassment of the act itself. We don't talk about it, so nobody should bring it up! When bringing someone home for the holidays or family gatherings, I ensured they already knew, so it wouldn't seem awkward the entire time when making the introductions. One time, my friend came to a family prayer meeting and said, "So your mom and dad are married to two different people? But you get to spend every holiday with them without having to leave?"

I laughed so hard and said, "Yes, that's true!"

It made me think of how grateful I was to have my parents with me at every family gathering. Although the relationship wasn't perfect, I had what most people didn't have.

Being able to share this about my parents has never affected me negatively. I told people that are close to me with ease because it's no big deal to me. I understand the bond they shared and how life circumstances and situations may or may not have contributed to it. So, talking about it was never hard. It is a part of who I am. I am not, nor will I ever be ashamed of who I am or where I come from, but I needed to talk about it...I just wanted a conversation. I'm not sure what it would've looked like, but I hadn't had a conversation with my parents since the first one. I had grown, matured, and learned a lot about myself through the things I experienced in my life, but they hadn't had an adult conversation with me.

For years, I allowed fear of rejection and pain to stop me from ever asking to have the conversation. Making the conscious decision to have THE conversation with my mom as an adult made me nervous, but it was necessary, and I'm glad it happened.

We sat down at the dining room table, and she said, "I will only speak for me because your dad is not here, and I will let him share his thoughts."

First, my mom reassured me of her love and how she was very proud of me. "I know the conversation is overdue, so I'm here to answer any questions you have for me."

I sat there fidgeting with my hands and trying not to seem nervous. At 26 years old, I sat in anticipation of getting answers to questions I've had since I was six years old.

"We never bonded as brother and sister. We took care of each other. We were in love."

Hearing those words from her didn't make me feel any better or worse about the situation—I just listened and tried to understand what she was saying like a sponge dipped in soapy water, soaking up every drop. I wanted to know; I needed to know. *Help me understand!* Help me understand how this happened and why?

To this day, I believe my parents still have a deep bond and connection that can never be broken! They met as teenagers and bonded as friends who gradually morphed into a deeper intimacy that can't be explained. If they could've been married, I believe they would have been.

So how do you explain this bond? Can you explain it? If we think back to the bible days, incest was normal, and no one frowned on it because it was how the earth was populated. Now hear me when I say this, I am in no way minimizing the act of incest itself or diminishing the fact that it has happened with force in some homes, and that is **not** ok.

I understand incest by rape and molestation has happened within many families, and I want you to know if that's you; I'm so sorry that happened to you. You can heal from this; you can move past it. But first, you must determine what healing from this looks like for you? I don't make light of the situation. I only make note that this was not that type of situation for my parents.

I am grateful for the life God gave me. Yet, sometimes, I would sit and visualize what my life would have been like with both of my parents in the same household. What it would be like to have a "normal life."

God gave me an amazing gift in the form of my beautiful mother. She is my world, and I thank God for placing her in my life. I am her twin, and we are alike in so many ways. I love it now, but I didn't as a child. Now I understand things a lot better. My perspective has shifted. The enemy tried to tear us apart for most of my life, putting a crack in our foundation.

Growing up, things were rocky with us. I never

understood why she was so angry all the time or where it came from. I love my mommy so much, and all I wanted was for her to love me unconditionally without the anger. I wanted her approval more than anything in this world. I watched her go through a very abusive marriage and learned she had been abused as a child. The cycle of the generational curses continued while everybody remained silent, never breaking the silence so that a space of vulnerability could be created and healing could happen.

When you think about your childhood, what types of emotions come to mind? Happy, joyful? Fun? If this is you, I'm so happy you experienced a pleasant childhood?

Unfortunately, not everyone associates childhood with playfulness and fun. If you experienced neglect, trauma, or other emotional pain, your inner child might seem small, vulnerable, and in need of protection. I know mine did, and you may have buried this pain deep to hide it and protect both your present self and the child you once were.

Hiding pain doesn't heal it. Instead, it often surfaces in your adult life, showing up as distress in personal relationships or difficulty meeting your own needs. Working to heal your inner child can help you address some of these issues. Healing your inner child can take time.

Will you join me?

Ok, Sis, let's check-in! How are you doing? I know there may be a few triggers as you read this book, so I do a mental health check-in at the end of every chapter. The purpose of this is to make you are more self-aware of your feelings and emotions.

This is an exercise that should be followed up with a therapist to help you process and begin to heal.

YOU GOOD, SIS MENTAL HEALTH CHECK-IN (TAKE A 15-20-MINUTE BREAK)

1. Pause, and take a deep breath
2. You good, Sis? (Ask yourself, am I ok? Do I need a break?) If so, put the book down and come back to it.
3. What did this chapter bring up for you?

4. Were you triggered? If so, let's explore it. Grab your journal, your favorite pen, get your blanket and let's write. Write what you felt; cry, release, and replace all negative beliefs with positive beliefs.

Chapter 2

Finding Monet

It's been a journey to "Find Mo." The "Monet" God says I am. I found myself adapting to the people around me throughout my entire life and being who they needed me to be. I never understood why being a "people pleaser" was so important to me. The desire to be accepted was a strong force in my life. I wanted to celebrate my friends in their special moments, i.e., birthdays, weddings, and baby showers. Whenever I was planning any event for my family and friends, I always went above and beyond to make sure everything was perfect for them. I felt strongly about serving people in whatever capacity THEY needed, but I was never a friend to myself. I genuinely enjoy seeing my friends and family celebrate their wins and special occasions.

I love to be the "hostess with mostess" of all the parties. I want other people to feel supported, loved, cherished, and appreciated, even if it means sacrificing my happiness, time, and money. Sometimes, knowing they wouldn't do it for me.

I didn't even know what loving myself looked like. I never put myself first. Although It gave me great joy to serve my friends, I desired to be celebrated and acknowledged by my peers.

For most of my adult life, the perceptions and opinions of others affected how I lived my life. It reminded me of how much I got lost in the little girl that just wanted to make her mommy happy and proud. I had a longing and a desire to have my mommy and my father's approval; *Anybody's* approval, for that matter.

Sometimes I felt like I could hear the people around me saying,

"She needs help."

"Something is wrong with her."

" Stay away from her."

"She's toxic! We don't know or understand her, but we just don't like her."

I felt that way in every circle I walked in throughout my adolescent years and my adult life. I always felt misunderstood, judged, and an outcast.

CONFLICT WITHOUT CONVERSATION

Since a young child, my heart's desire has been to be a "virtuous woman." I wanted to be the "First Lady" and walk in the footsteps of my grandmothers. Growing up in a family of pastors, ministers, singers, and even musicians, I was taught the word of God. We memorized scriptures, learned how to pray, and lean on God, and, of course, we are a family of worshippers! Therefore, I knew how to go to God, get on my face and turn my plate over when I experienced hardships. But not the professional tools combined with it. I didn't have the guidance on dealing with the effects of the trauma I had experienced. My dad took my sister and me to therapy/counseling. We started counseling, stopped counseling, and didn't go back, but the few times we did go, it was to a family friend who was a therapist. She left such a lasting impression on me, reminding me that I am fearfully and wonderfully made. She bought my sister and me a mirror and showed us how to repeat affirmations to ourselves daily. We did one-on-one and group. This is what helped me to embrace counseling as an adult.

I struggled with internal thoughts that had me in turmoil because there were always elephants in the rooms in my family. I needed us to have the conversation. Yes, *thee* conversation to explain the behavior that everyone gossiped about.

*We're so disappointed in you...*but NEVER the CONVERSATION... *we don't support you because you were not raised this way...* But NEVER the CONVERSATION... *She is in jail again? She's pregnant at 19, again at 21, and* *again at 22. WOW! 3 KIDS not married before the age of 23. Why doesn't she just be obedient?* But NEVER THE CONVERSATION...

I had experienced abuse, rejection, even sexual perversions but never received the conversation I so desperately needed— the conversation that could've changed my life and view of the world. My heart longed for both of my parents to speak to me about all of this, and it could've shown me what real love looked like, what support meant, and how being vulnerable and transparent could shift how you show up in your life.

I felt as if everyone was looking at my impulsive behaviors and anger outbursts to my siblings but not ever exploring the option of the root cause of why those things happened. Sometimes we focus on the behaviors or responses the child gives to a situation more than *why* they respond that way.

My heart also desired a conversation with my family about how and why this relationship happened, resulting not in one but two children. As intrigued and interested as I was, I really wanted to know how to prevent it from happening again. I began to ask some questions to my parents and grandparents as I got older. My parents and grandparents gave me their perspective about what happened and how it happened. As I said before, I have never been embarrassed about my parents because I've always felt that I wouldn't be here if God didn't allow it. God doesn't make mistakes. I know I am here for a purpose. Jeremiah 1:5 says, " Before I formed thee in the belly I knew thee; and before thou camest forth out of the womb I sanctified thee, and I ordained thee a prophet unto the nations." This scripture tells me the unique circumstances around how I was born were in God's Perfect Will for my life. That's all I needed to know.

It was comforting to me to learn that our experiences are not our own. We go through things to help other people. I don't see the point in being shamed for it or feeling guilty because of the circumstances of how it happened. I just wish we had the conversation.

The elephants were always in the room; I needed answers about more than just incest. What is going on in our family? We needed to have some honest conversations about generational curses, abuse, forgiveness, self-image, and more. *Why didn't we talk?* I know this isn't just my family, but yours too. Everyone needs to have these complex, honest conversations, and not just the surface work or the cycle will continue. I understand some things are personal and private to each family member, and some may not be in the position to speak about the issue and a host of other explanations. But we must take the first steps to stand together as a family against the spiritual attacks and warfare.

Growing up a pastor's granddaughter, people had ideas and expectations of who we were, what we did, and how we lived. The attention is always on you, and I felt like we needed to keep the perception going. I love God and going to church, but I never liked pretentious people, and I could see right through them; it annoyed me and caused me to pull back from the church.

Codependency

My friendships were crucial to me, and I started looking for acceptance from them. I am a "people person" who loves networking and meeting new people, but sometimes it wasn't easy for me to let people in;

but when I did, I loved hard. When you love "hard," sometimes you can get hurt "hard."

When you are lost in life's journey to find yourself and unsure of who you are, it's easy to adapt your friend's mannerisms, behaviors, and even perspectives. That's what happened with my closest friends and me; We loved and depended on each other.

Friends were important to me because what I needed in my life, honesty, love, and authenticity, was lacking. I felt I could find that through friendships and relationships.

So, it truly hurt me when some of my childhood relationships didn't survive adulthood. But I have come to learn that people are in your life for reasons and seasons, and you can't grow with certain people still attached to you.

In my quest to "Find Mo," I looked for love in all the wrong places. I just wanted to feel loved and accepted by my peers. Let me show you what codependency in friendships looks like. My best friend and I stayed on Facetime for hours and hours during the day because we didn't want to miss moments out of each other's life. When we first met, we clicked immediately; kindred spirits. We bonded on many levels and started going to each other's houses almost every day. A few weeks later, we received a prophetic word while being prayed for at a fellow church member's house that our friendship would be like "iron sharpening iron;" we would always be connected. We took those words and ran with them, especially after how quickly our relationship had happened. We both had a desire to be needed, valued, appreciated, and acknowledged. We didn't recognize the codependency in the relationship immediately. We fell out, reconnected, fell out again, and reconnected again. The toxicity level of this relationship was at an all-time high in everybody else's eyes. Although we couldn't see it, we consistently found our way back to each other. Our friendship was the perfect example of hurt people hurting people, as the saying goes.

Being friends with her showed me a different life I hadn't seen before. This exposure made me hope for more in my life. I do know that our relationship was divinely connected even though one day, we were arguing, and the next, we were friends. We had a back-and-forth rollercoaster of a relationship, but I loved it, loved her. I never felt like I belonged in her world. My world was so opposite, and I didn't know how to handle it. I self-sabotaged for that reason.

As time went on, we realized we could have a healthy relationship. We both made a conscious decision to have an honest conversation. This allowed us to forgive each other, create healthy boundaries, and begin the healing process.

Life is funny.

How did I even allow myself to be in a codependent friendship? I realized I was constantly self-sabotaging myself for fear of rejection. I was used to certain behaviors and outcomes in my life, and what and who was comfortable. The reality is I was not emotionally ready for an authentic relationship. I had "friends," even "best friends," but none of my friendships had been like this.

Pete Walker says in his book Complex PTSD: From Surviving to Thriving,

"The definition of trauma-based codependency—a syndrome of self-abandonment and self-abnegation. Codependency is a fear-based inability to express rights, needs, and boundaries in relationships. It is a disorder of assertiveness characterized by a dormant fight response and a susceptibility to being exploited, abused, and or neglected."

In hindsight, I realize the betrayal I experienced from my friends changed my perspective on friendship and how I viewed myself. This forced me to reevaluate my life, friendships, and relationships.

In that reevaluation, I found myself and what I wanted for myself. I started self-reflecting, acknowledging, and accepting myself for who I was becoming. This made me more aware. I went to therapy, and while in counseling, I began to heal from all the hurt I experienced. So, my perceptions changed from how I saw *all* of my relationships. Sometimes we can see something one way, and someone else perceives it differently. Neither of us is wrong. They are both valid experiences, and I learned that we could agree to disagree and move forward.

TRAUMA RESPONSES

So much has changed in my life since this journey started. I began to build healthy boundaries and not take everything so personally. When you have been repetitively traumatized in childhood, you learn to survive by overusing one or two of the 4F Responses. Fight, Flight, Freeze, or Fawn. There are positive and negative characteristics associated with these responses. (see insert) I have responded with all of these. Right now, I am speaking about the fight response. The fight response is referred to as a bully. The unconscious belief is that power and control can create safety, assuage abandonment, and secure love. I learned that I needed to have control because I didn't have it as a child. I wanted to control my relationships because they made me feel safe and secure. This part of me was hard to accept because I never liked that version of me, but I had a hard time relinquishing control. I had to be in control of everything around me. When you grow up in a consistent survival state, you thrive on having control. Sometimes it's a good thing to be in control of your life, but not to the point where you control everything and everyone around you.

UNLEARNING BAD BEHAVIOR

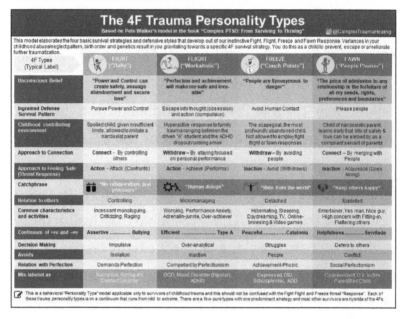

The 4F Trauma Personality Types
Based on Pete Walker's model in the book "Complex PTSD: From Surviving to Thriving" @ComplexTraumaHealing

This model elaborates the four basic survival strategies and defensive styles that develop out of our instinctive Fight, Flight, Freeze and Fawn Response. Variances in your childhood abuse/neglect pattern, birth order and genetics result in you gravitating towards a specific 4F survival strategy. You do this as a child to prevent, escape or ameliorate further traumatization.

4F Types (Typical Label)	FIGHT ("Bully")	FLIGHT ("Workaholic")	FREEZE ("Couch Potato")	FAWN ("People Pleaser")
Unconscious Belief	"Power and Control can create safety, assuage abandonment and secure love"	"Perfection and achievement will make me safe and loveable"	"People are Synonymous to danger"	"The price of admission to any relationship is the forfeiture of all my needs, rights, preferences and boundaries"
Ingrained Defense Survival Pattern	Pursue Power and Control	Escape into thought (obsession) and action (compulsion)	Avoid Human Contact	Please people
Childhood contributing environment	Spoiled child, given insufficient limits, allowed to imitate a narcissist parent	Hyperactive response to family trauma ranging between the driven "A" student and the ADHD dropout running amok	The scapegoat, the most profoundly abandoned child. Not allowed to employ fight, flight or fawn responses	Child of narcissistic parent learns early that bits of safety & love can be earned by as a compliant servant of parents
Approach to Connection	Connect – By controlling others	Withdraw – By staying focused on personal performance	Withdraw – By avoiding people	Connect – By merging with People
Approach to Feeling Safe (Threat Response)	Action - Attack (Confronts)	Action - Achieve (Performs)	Inaction - Avoid (Withdraws)	Inaction - Acquiesce (Goes Along)
Catchphrase	"No relationships, just prisoners"	"Human doings"	"Hide from the world"	"Keep others happy"
Relation to others	Controlling	Micromanaging	Detached	Exploited
Common characteristics and activities	Incessant monologuing, Criticizing, Raging	Worrying, Performance Anxiety, Adrenalin-junkie, Over-achiever	Hibernating, Sleeping, Daydreaming, TV, Online-browsing & Video games	Entertainer, Yes man, Nice guy, High concern with Fitting-in, Flattering others
Continuum of +ve and –ve	Assertive .... Bullying	Efficient .... Type A	Peaceful............Catatonia	Helpfulness............Servitude
Decision Making	Impulsive	Over-analytical	Struggles	Defers to others
Avoids	Isolation	Inaction	People	Conflict
Relation with Perfection	Demands Perfection	Compelled by Perfectionism	Achievement-Phobic	Social Perfectionism
Mis labeled as	Narcissist, Sociopath, Conduct Disorder	OCD, Mood Disorder (Bipolar), ADHD	Depressed, DID, Schizophrenic, ADD	Codependent D.V. Victim, Parentified Child

This is a behavioral "Personality Type" model applicable only to survivors of childhood trauma and this should not be confused with the Fight Flight and Freeze threat "Response". Each of these trauma personality types is on a continuum that runs from mild to extreme. There are a few pure types with one predominant strategy and most other survivors are hybrids of the 4Fs.

Now, I manage my emotions and my impulses better. Even though it's been a rocky road, I am thankful to have found the Monet that I am proud of. I walk boldly in the authority God has given me. I embrace my failures and use them to propel me forward into the next phase of my life. I learned what my triggers are and how to respond to those triggers. When you know better, you do better, so I surround myself with accountability partners to ensure I stay on the right path to success and healing.

Monet as the mom of girls is the version that is still evolving, but I am learning to be patient with her. Because I am determined to break the cycle and have the necessary conversations with my daughters, I had a conversation with my oldest daughter about her experience while I was in a domestic violence relationship (which I will discuss in detail later), and it breaks my heart to hear her talk about being scared for me. The majority of the time we fought or argued, we "thought" the girls were asleep but obviously, although they didn't come out of the room to check on what was happening, they heard it. Camille is the only one that remembers specific times where things were bad. Unfortunately, she remembers the worst of them.

She said, "Mama, I wasn't sleeping all the time. I was scared, so I pretended to be asleep."

She wanted to help me. My heart just sunk. I didn't know what to say besides apologize to her, hug, and affirm that none of that was her fault. I knew I had to make some real changes quickly because statistics show 1 in 4 women will experience domestic violence. I refused to allow any one of my four daughters to be a part of that statistic.

I started to focus my attention on making sure I was showing Camille how to unlearn what she had heard and may be seen. She is just like me, the oldest, and we are alike in many ways, but she is so strong, even now at her young age. Resilience comes as second nature to her. It's so refreshing to see your children build resilience and strength to get through the hard things in their childhood, but it's painful to see what causes them to have to do it.

Nevertheless, I have learned this is part of the journey and her story. All I can do is continue to unlearn the toxic traits, push forward in therapy and be the best mother God called me to be for them. My four daughters are my why and my motivation.

Camille is my reminder that I broke that generational curse off our bloodlines, and it comes with daily practices of forgiveness, grace, and patience. But the work was not complete; I had a few more curses to break off my bloodline for my children. Motherhood is a journey, but it's one of the greatest journeys you will take. Embrace the responsibility of not passing on toxic behaviors to your children. Walk in the peace that God gives, and He will provide you with guidance along the way. You are the Mom; God gave your children for a reason. Don't take the blessing of being a mom for granted by not giving it all you got. Have hard, important conversations with your children.

Hold yourself accountable if you were wrong and move on. It's ok to say, "I'm sorry," and show them you are human and still make mistakes. If they are old enough to understand, explain why certain things happened and how they can choose a different path. I have always been transparent with my children about the decisions I have made and the relationships and friendships I chose. I decided to share my experiences and failures with my children so they understood early how not to fall into the same temptations I did. Sometimes all our children want is for us to be open and honest with them about our shortcomings and life lessons to show them we can relate. Our children are extremely resilient and understand a lot more than we think. Don't count them out! Let's help build a healthy foundation for the generation of our grandchildren.

Some conversations are difficult, like the one coming up in my next chapter, but I also disclosed that to my children. I refuse to keep perpetuating the unhealthy tradition of silence, and I will have the conversation.

You good, Sis Mental Health Check-in (Take a 15–20-minute break)

1. Pause, and take a deep breath
2. You good, Sis? (Ask yourself, am I ok? Do I need a break?) If so, put the book down and come back to it.
3. What did this chapter bring up for you?
4. Were you triggered? If so, let's explore it. Grab your journal, your favorite pen, get your blanket and let's write. Write what you felt; cry, release, and replace all negative beliefs with positive beliefs.

Chapter 3

Spn: 02345594 - Harris County Jail

My heart is racing, walking slowly but swiftly to the exit. Five steps out the door, a young lady who had just purchased a coke grabbed my basket and calmly said, "Ma'am, please step back inside the building. I'm with Walmart loss prevention, and I need you to come with me."

"No, I am not coming back with you."

I started walking away. Then there was a guy who approached me. I saw this guy in the store, but I never knew he was a part of loss prevention. They had me surrounded and wouldn't allow me to leave. I didn't fight or attempt to run; I simply followed them to the office and waited as they called the police.

How do I explain this to my girls? Today was Saturday, my nephew's birthday party, and I was stealing clothes for them to wear and other miscellaneous household needs. How am I going to explain to my family that I would be in jail again for stealing? I knew they would keep me this time because it was my third offense for theft.

I was sitting there scared and shaking as they sat there talking about me so horribly. I knew I didn't have to do this. I felt worse listening to this young black dude telling me the same thing. He said that I didn't have to do this, and this was beneath me. They said the lady watched me from the time I walked into the store to the time I tried to leave.

They allowed me to make a phone call. I called my children's father to tell him what was going on and to let my family know. They were expecting me to come back for the party.

I'm going to jail for a while this time, I thought, then cried like a baby. Soon anxiety crept in, and I became terrified. I was a struggling single mom, a full-time student with a criminal background, and I was just trying to survive and take care of my girls. I didn't have any consistent help. It always fell on me to figure it out... and that's my specialty figuring it out, no matter what.

I would regularly go to different Walmarts to steal, and I got away more times than I was caught. Each time I said to myself, "After this, I am done stealing. I can control this, and I have to figure something else out."

Yet here I was again.

I thought of all of this as I sat in a cold and disgusting jail cell with many other women of different ethnicities, backgrounds, and ages. The spirit of abandonment came over me, and I felt so alone in a room full of people. People were everywhere, lying all over the ground with some tissue as their pillow. Some were lying over on the benches with their faces on their hands tucked inside of their clothes because it was so cold. The phones didn't have receivers, so you had to put your ear up to the speaker, causing everyone to be loud and talk over each other.

That same night I went to Harris County Probable Cause Court. I needed a bond, and I wanted to hear that I would get a Personal Recognizance bond, but I knew I didn't qualify. My next hope was to receive a bond low enough so that I could bond out.

I went to Probable Cause Court, and the judge Mirandized me. They gave me a 30k bond, and I needed 10% to get out. As I was sitting in the back of the courtroom waiting to go back to the holding cell, I thought, *I don't have that type of money, and this was my third offense,* so I got even more nervous. But all I could do was wait until Monday for my court date.

I went back to the holding cell and called my children's father to update him. Even though I had been to jail before, this time was worse because the stakes were higher. I did not know what to expect. Not to mention the overwhelming guilt and disappointment I felt in myself.

That same night after Probable Cause Court, I remember wanting to hear my name called to go home.

"Cullins," the guard called.

I jumped up and ran to the door, hoping to be released or bonded out. Instead, she told me I was going upstairs to Housing. Going upstairs is what you don't want to do; that means you are not going home any time soon. I grabbed my papers from the Probable Cause Court and slowly walked towards the guard.

All the inmates lined up one behind the other, and I remember walking the halls to the elevator thinking, *I can't believe I am back here again. I can't believe I did this again.*

"Turn around and face the wall, shoulder to shoulder. No talking," the guards said to us as we walked into the elevator.

Walking down the hall, I was triggered by the sounds, smells, and the same feelings I felt the previous times I had been to jail. *Why do I keep doing this over and over again? Just a week ago, we celebrated my decision to be obedient, follow God, and move to Dallas. Now I am sitting in jail.*

43

At 3 am Monday, I heard my name being called for court. I had to get up and prepare myself mentally and physically for court. A few other inmates and I were escorted into a gym, where we all had to be stripped and searched before sitting in a holding cell for hours. This process is the worse because you are excited about going to court, hoping to hear good news, but it's an all-day event. I can't even describe how humiliating it is to go through this. I just wanted to go home and be with my girls.

During court, all of us inmates were all waiting to hear our names called by our lawyers and the words, "You can go home today with time served."

Unfortunately, only two of us heard those words, and I was not one of them. I sat in the back, curled up with my hands in my face praying to God harder than I ever have before. I was begging Him to get me out of this situation, telling Him I would never do it again. However, the words I would soon hear would change my life forever.

The cell was very small, with a glass window for us to speak with our attorney through. I couldn't afford to get an attorney on my own, so I was given a court-appointed attorney. A black woman came to the glass and said, "DeShandra Cullins, Hi, I'm your attorney; how are you?"

"I could be better."

"This is your 3rd offense. The judge wants you to serve 3 months minimum. You have a few days that can be used towards your sentence, but you will serve out the rest of your sentence. I'm sorry this is the final offer the D.A. is going to give; however, you have the option to bail out. Let me see if the judge will lower your bail, so you can get home to your daughters."

"Thank you so much for helping me."

"You're welcome, but I don't want to see you back in here. Your girls need you, and this is no place for you."

As I heard these words coming from the lips of my attorney, I thought, *wow, thank you, Lord, for giving me a compassionate attorney*. Many public defenders I have been in contact with don't care about you or your family. They only care about solving the case expeditiously. *You can't back out from this, Mo*, I thought. I must go through this storm. *What did I get myself into?!*

"What are my options?"

She said she would reset my court date after I post bail, allowing me to leave jail and return in 30 days to serve my sentence. However, the resetting continued for about 5 months, and then I was told that I would have to surrender myself in December. At this time, I was living in Dallas because I moved there in August of 2014. But I had to return to Houston and turn myself in.

This was one of the hardest things I have had to deal with. I had never been away from my children longer than a few days. I cried and cried for weeks before I turned myself in. I'm so grateful to my village, who stepped up and helped take care of my children while I was away.

On December 8, 2014, I made a huge breakfast, played with the girls for a little while, then their dad dropped our children off with their aunt and uncle so he could drop me off. My heart was hurting to leave them there, but I knew I was DONE with shoplifting after this. A few hours later, I turned myself over to the courts to serve out my 60-day sentence in Harris County Jail.

How did I get here? I had nothing but time to think about my decisions and the consequences of those decisions.

An Unexpected Thrill

It started when I was a kid.

The earliest age I can remember stealing was at the age of 10. I was at the store with my dad and his girlfriend at the time. We went to get food for tacos. I wanted some Bubblicious Bubble gum, but my dad wouldn't get it for me. So, I stuck it in my pocket, and when it was time to leave, I walked out of the store.

I remember the tingling feeling in my stomach, sweaty palms, and inner WOW! It was such a rush. I felt good, and I felt the excitement that I had gotten away with something. This was my first time experiencing impulsivity, and it was great until I got caught. I was helping put the bags in the car, and the gum fell out of my pocket.

My dad asked, "Where did you get that? I told you no, you couldn't have that."

"From the store," I mumbled.

Sighing heavily, he asked, "DeShandra, why do you keep doing this?"

"I don't know," came out so softly, like a whisper.

We went back inside the store, and he told the manager what I had done. The manager told me he would not press charges, but I should be lucky to have a father like him. I felt horrible because I knew I had disappointed my dad. But I did not understand why I "enjoyed" doing this so much. Apparently, from my dad's response, I had done this more than one time before this, but this is the memory that sticks out the most.

IMPULSIVITY AND TRAUMA

The professionals say impulsivity is a trauma response. I was extremely impulsive—not only in stealing but in other areas of my life like sexually, financially, and with food. If I had a craving, I had to satisfy it immediately. No matter what it was or what it took to satisfy it. Come hell or high water, I was doing it. I felt like I was just putting a Band-Aid on the womb instead of dealing with it. I knew the decisions I was making weren't a representation of what God called me to do, but it was hard to shake.

I remember having a dream consistently for three years straight of me driving a vehicle, and no matter where I went, no matter the location, I drove the same speed limit. In the dream, I was wildly out of control. My car would go well over 100 mph, but it would never crash. I remember seeing and feeling like that was a comparison to my life spinning out of control. I allowed my impulses to make decisions for me. I rested comfortably in the impulsivity to avoid dealing with the problem, forgiving myself, and moving forward.

Often we get so wrapped up in instant gratification and having things the way we want them that we don't see the unhealthy habits that can cause impulsivity. I am not saying that impulsivity and trauma caused me to steal. Those were decisions that I made; I had a choice, and so do you with your decisions.

Our experiences play a part in our upbringing and affect our view of life and our decision-making. We have to take responsibility for the part we play in our life. God gives us free will to make our own decisions. Accountability is key. We don't want to be bystanders but active participants in our lives. So, with that being the case, no longer do I blame people for my impulses. I don't even blame my trauma. Although I know it plays a major role in my behavior. I have learned to take responsibility for my actions, forgive myself, make better choices and help others.

Blessings in the Lessons

Sitting in that jail cell from December 8, 2014-February 4, 2015, changed my life forever. I missed moments with my children I can never get back. It was an eye-opening experience for me. I learned so much about who I was, the choices I made, and the type of mother I wanted to become. Even while being in a jail cell, God was dealing with me the entire time. I started journaling, and the Holy Spirit told me to write a book and my life experiences would minister to others.

I was determined to use my last time incarcerated to change my life. So, I started reading my bible every day and going to chapel when they had it. Worship was always just what I needed to get me through the rest of the week. I met so many people while in jail, and most of them in my cell block knew I was writing my book. A few of us got really close and gave each other nicknames. They called me "Pretty."

"Pretty, did you write today?" They made sure I got it done.

I used to worship despite the loud noises throughout the cell block. I would start singing out loud,

"I love you, Jesus, I worship and adore you, I just want to tell you... Lord, I love you. more than anything!"

Those songs stayed in my spirit the entire time I was in jail. When I felt down, I would start giving praises to God. The Bible says in Psalm 34:1, I will bless the Lord at all times, and His praise shall continually be in my mouth.

Even while sitting in a jail cell, I learned to wake up with gratitude and praise on my lips. It shifted the entire atmosphere around me. Sometimes I would just walk around the walls of the cell, which had about 20 beds in it, and just pray and worship until God comforted me at that moment. I was reminded how God is the God of ALL comfort, which includes being in jail, feeling sad, depressed, and in pain. He can comfort you right where you are. All you have to do is trust Him and believe in His ability to see you through it.

My cellmates and I built a bond, and I'm so grateful for those I met and had a chance to have an impact on. When you are in jail, it's hard to trust people you don't know with intimate details of your life or situation, but you can definitely go to God in prayer, and He will answer.

You can literally be whoever you want to be in jail. People produce all kinds of stories about their "outside world" life that are simply not true. But I met a few genuine people I am still in contact with today, and God has also transformed them. When I think about my experience in jail, I think of Paul, Joseph, Samson, Daniel, John, and even Jesus himself. Jesus was held in custody between His arrest, crucifixion, and death. It reminds me that we are not perfect, and God can and will still use us!

I remember waking up every morning counting down the days until I heard "ATW," which means "All the way" out the door! I made a calendar on the back of the tablet to cross off the days as they slowly passed. I talked to my girls every day, sometimes more than once, because it was tough some days, especially on my daughter Chloe's birthday, Christmas, New Year, and several days in between. Talking to them helped calm my anxiety and gave me peace of mind knowing they were safe while mommy was at "work." Unfortunately, I couldn't tell them the truth then, it was too much for me to digest at the time, so I was not ready to share that side with them. But I thank God for not only allowing me to be vulnerable with my girls about my shortcomings and why I made those decisions but the ability to teach them so that they understand the consequences of their actions. I want my girls to see me fall and be human, but always recognize where I was wrong, correct it and then get back up better than before.

PRAYER TO BREAK THE CURSE

Failure is inevitable, but success you must work for, and it comes with growth. When it comes to things in families, some of us feel that if grandma and our mother did it, then it's ok." It's easier to just accept things the way they are, but you have to choose to want differently for your bloodline. Several generational curses have been broken off of my bloodline through consistent prayer and fasting. They can be broken off of yours too!

Let's pray together and break the curses off of your bloodline! The sins of the fathers are simply confessed away by the Believer and a close friend and prayer partner. So before praying this prayer, grab your prayer partner and let us pray.

Almighty Father, In Jesus Name, by the power of the Holy Spirit, I, by an act of my will, sever the sins of my forefathers and declare they no longer have influence in my life (and the life of my children) Enemy, in the Name of Jesus you can no longer attack my (our) mind, will, emotions, my body, oppress my spirit, my daily walk, my Christian walk, what I have or may have in the future. By confession before heaven and this witness, I break these generational curses off my entire family line now and forever. We are free.

The Friend Confirms:

Father, I witness and attest to this prayer and record at (time, month, and date) (Believers Name) has by an act of his/her will severed the influence of the sins of the fathers in his/her (Children's) life and all future generations in Jesus' name. Amen

You good, Sis Mental Health Check-in (Take a 15–20-minute break)

1. Pause, and take a deep breath

2. You good, Sis? (Ask yourself, am I ok? Do I need a break?) If so, put the book down and come back to it.

3. What did this chapter bring up for you?

4. Were you triggered? If so, let's explore it. Grab your journal, your favorite pen, get your blanket and let's write. Write what you felt; cry, release, and replace all negative beliefs with positive beliefs.

Chapter 4

Love and Abuse

We met on the phone and talked for three years before we met in person. He lived on the Northside of Houston, and I lived in Alief on Houston's Southwest side. My mother wouldn't let me anywhere near a boy, so I chose to sneak. His cousin lived in my neighborhood and went to my school, so that is how we met. I was 14, he was 15, and he was my first love. We talked for hours on the phone. For years, Myspace and Blackplanet were our main lines of communication before we met in person. He revealed his trauma to me early in our relationship, and we were trauma-bonded based on our similar childhood experiences. It was harder for us to separate from each other because of what we had gone through. We knew it wasn't a healthy situation, but we stayed; however, we fought often. I wanted us to learn how to *unlearn* abusive behavior together.

We finally met in person after I graduated high school. I will never forget sitting in the car in his parent's driveway with my best friend, nervous about getting out of the car. It was dark outside, and he was sitting in front of his house. I remember the huge dimples on his face. He had the biggest smile when he saw me. My heart melted, and I fell in love even more. I loved his smile and everything about him! We had dinner, laughed, and talked all night. I stayed with him that night, and our bond became deeper.

After a while, I left to attend college in Dallas, so we were apart for some time. During our hiatus, I got involved with Camille's father. I became pregnant, but that relationship didn't work out. My mom picked us up from the hospital shortly after they discharged Camille. Camille was born at thirty weeks and was in the NICU for two months. This was a very tough time for me. Later, when I returned to Houston, me and my first love got back together.

After about six months of being back home in Houston, I moved out of my mom's house and into an apartment with my sisters. Each one ended up going their own way and left me in the apartment that I couldn't afford by myself, so I was evicted.

I stayed with a friend and his family for a few months, and then my mom got an apartment for me in her name, and I was on my own again. I became pregnant with my second child Cayleigh so I invited my "abuser" to move in so we could be a family. I will refer to my first love as my abuser from here on out in this chapter because the love turned into abuse.

We were finally living out the dream we had talked about for years as teenagers. Things were going so well. We were excited about a new baby and ready to start this new journey of our lives! I was so excited to be with a man I knew understood me, what I had been through, and always accepted me!

Towards the end of my pregnancy, I started to see the dark side of him. He became very jealous and controlling. One time, he thought I was texting someone else, and he got so angry. We argued, and he punched a hole in the closet door. I was frozen and triggered. He didn't hit me, but I was scared and didn't know what would happen next because I had been through abuse before. This was the first time he reacted this way, so I made excuses for his behavior. We talked about it and moved on.

If I am honest with myself, I would tell you how I noticed the signs early on during our phone calls over the years. I noticed how he spoke to me and how it made me feel. However, I ignored it because it was "normal" to me. I brushed it off and blamed the way we were raised as an excuse. I wanted to help him.

So, we got past the punch in the wall. But I noticed I started being aggressive and provoking him in certain situations also. I was on edge and angry all the time. It was like that trigger lasted for years, and I began to act in survival mode. The more our relationship continued, the worse it got. There were some really good moments and some really bad ones. There were times after we argued and fought that I would just sit in the bed and cry. Not just because of the situation but because we promised each other to be better. We didn't want to repeat the same things our parents did.

I wanted to fix it, but it seemed like the more we tried, the more we hurt each other. We never tried to go to counseling or get outside help other than family and friends, and they didn't help the situation much. The fact of the matter is, we were not good for each other. Unfortunately, my understanding of this came after counseling and after leaving the relationship.

TRAUMA BONDING

Through counseling, I understood that we had trauma bonded. Our relationship was not the "traditional" domestic violence relationship because, in our relationship, we both were the aggressor. Having both experienced traumas in our childhood, we had a deep trauma bond and an unhealthy soul-tie due to having sex before marriage. However, we had no idea a trauma bond existed or how to break the unhealthy soul tie. We hurt each other over and over again.

Trauma bonds are real, and not enough people understand the power they possess in an unhealthy relationship. There are seven stages of trauma bonding, and if you are in this type of relationship, you must get counseling to get the help you need.

If it is physically abusive and you are the abuser, stop right now, seek forgiveness, and leave the relationship until you can be healthy for your partner.

Trauma bonding makes you psychologically addicted to your abuser, and you can start to feel anxiety just from the idea of having to leave the relationship. The thought of leaving can make you physically feel like it's impossible. It's an addictive cycle that continues until it's broken by one or both people in the relationship. Many of us have or are currently experiencing trauma bonding in relationships due to seeing that behavior as a child or being in an abusive relationship and not going to counseling. Hence you repeat that cycle in your next relationship.

I want you to know I'm not judging you; I've been there, and whether you are on the receiving end or giving end, you can change the trajectory of your life, but you must recognize it first.

Here are the seven stages of trauma bonding:

1. **Love bombing**
2. **Trust and Codependency**
3. **Criticism**
4. **Manipulation/Gaslighting**
5. **Giving up control**
6. **Losing yourself**
7. **Addiction to the cycle**

MORE ABUSE

The next incident that stands out to me is when we were driving to one of my best friends' house for a fight party, and he got upset because I said something smart, and he punched me in my mouth. I hit him back, and he started swerving the car. He pulled over, and I started yelling at him. "I can't believe you hit me in my mouth!!" We argued about whose fault it was and then eventually let it go.

We still went to my friend's house that night. I cried the entire way there, and I was no longer in a mood to "have fun." But I managed to put a smile on my face and walk in like nothing had happened. My friend saw that my lip was swollen, and we went into her bathroom.

"Mo, again? When are you going to stop doing this with him? You don't deserve this. What happened this time?"

I explained the story.

"Sis, I'm so sorry." And she hugged me as I wailed in her arms from the enormous amount of emotional pain I felt. Sure, my body was tired, but emotionally, I was so tired; Tired of being "abused' by anyone." I just wanted to feel peace in my relationship and be genuinely happy.

It seems as if holidays and other special days were the worst. Even though I love holidays and birthdays, I started to hate having them because I dreaded the arguments, fights, and calling the cops. There was always an issue with us. One of the breaking points was when I realized my mental health was affected, and I didn't want to feel the pain anymore.

I started to self-medicate with Tylenol PM and wine just so I couldn't feel the pain. It worked for a little while, but then I needed something stronger. I started smoking weed, and eventually, I would use all three at one time. A few years after being in and out of this relationship, I finally got the strength to "leave him." I moved into an apartment with my girls, and he moved into an apartment not too far from me. I thought, *Yes, this is it! I am free, I am not going back, I can do this.*

I was working at Houston Community College, driving a brand-new Dodge Journey, and it was just the girls and me. I was so proud of myself! I would get up, get them ready, drop them off at daycare, and head to work/school. I was doing the damn thing! (Sorry, Mama) I was a single mother, but I was "doing good" on the outside, anyway. I was making things happen without hearing what I wasn't doing right! I felt like I was dying inside and on autopilot going through the motions but not actually present in my children's lives. I let him come back a few times, put him out, and did the dance again. Until one day, I felt like I couldn't handle it anymore. I had been dealing with depression and anxiety since childhood. Still, I didn't know how to get the help I needed without getting on medication, so I never tried. I had heard such horrible things about the medication, so I wasn't interested. Until the day I attempted to take my own life.

TIRED OF BEING TIRED

We had just gotten into a huge argument; he broke my phone again, and I had had enough! So, I went into the bathroom and took a handful of Tylenol pm. As I put them in my mouth, my abuser walked in and tackled me to the ground, trying to get the pills out of my mouth. I fought him and tried to swallow as many as I could before he got any out. My best friend since 6th grade was living with me at the time, came in from work, and ran in the room screaming, "What are you doing?"

My abuser screamed while wrestling with me, "She took a lot of pills."

She yelled, "Where is the bottle?" and immediately called 911. She told them I had taken a lot of pills, but she didn't know how many.

When we got to the hospital, I remember the nurses asking me how I was feeling, whether I intentionally took the pills and whether I was suicidal? As tears rolled down my face, I paused and nodded my head. The nurse said I have to hear you say it. Overwhelmed, I managed to get out, "Yes."

"Okay, are things bad at home?"

And it was a trigger for me as a child when the school nurses would ask me that after they saw a bruise on me.

"No, it's fine. I just have a lot going on."

"Okay, we're going to have to send you to a facility to see a psychiatrist that can help you."

"No, ma'am, I just want to go home; I don't need to go there."

"Unfortunately, this isn't an option; we are mandated by law to make sure you are safe and properly cared for after a suicide attempt. They will evaluate you and determine how long you have to stay; it may not belong. Still, they can help you."

I immediately started to blame myself for making a "stupid" decision. I heard the voices of people close to me, when they heard I tried to commit suicide, say, *She's just doing that for attention; she will be ok!* Those words stuck with me long after because I thought, *maybe I am just dramatic. Maybe it's not as bad as it seems.* As time passed, I thought, well, yes, it is for attention, just not the attention they were referring to. It's a cry for help! We have to start paying attention to the signs of mental health disorders and start taking them seriously!

Our people are dying for fear of being judged or it being brushed away like a common cold. Taking care of our mental health and our relationship with Christ go hand in hand. We must nurture and talk about them both, and we must create a safe space to talk about mental health and Jesus often.

I was in the psychiatric hospital for a week and a half, and I felt like I didn't belong there. I was completely stripped of my privacy. I missed my daughters, and I just wanted to go home. I started to see the Psychiatrist so I could unpack what I was feeling. She diagnosed me as being severely depressed since my childhood due to childhood trauma. I agreed with her, and I told her I felt like this my entire life, but it seemed to have gotten worse when I had postpartum depression with each of my children. I didn't know you could be depressed as a child until she said it. She knew I was adamant about not taking medication, so she explained the benefits and the risks of the antidepressant she prescribed because it would help balance the chemicals in my brain and start going to therapy because they work hand in hand. She also reminded me I couldn't leave the hospital until I started taking the medication. So, I started taking the medication and started therapy. I saw a difference after a month or so, but I was not consistent in my therapy, so neither one worked. I started feeling depressed again and went back to my abusive relationship for another two years before leaving for good. This trauma bond had us welded together, and I couldn't shake him.

My mental health was not a priority for me; I didn't know it needed to be. I thought I just had to figure it out. "You'll be fine, girl; You have been through worse than this; Just pray about it, and it will be ok."

No ma'am, No sir. God put medication, therapists, psychiatrists, and other doctors here on this earth for us to use them! Your mental health doctor (therapist/

psychiatrist/counselor) is just as important as your primary care physician and gynecologist. Your mind controls your body in so many ways; it has the power to wake you from anesthesia during surgery. If nothing else works, doctors will depend on you to wake up.

When you prioritize your mental health, you are stronger. When you think of the physical fight or flight response, think about this scenario. When you're stressed or anxious, your body reacts as if it is under attack. Your body releases hormones that speed up your heart rate, breathing, increases blood pressure, and make your muscles tense. This is just from a "feeling" or "emotion" that indicates stress.

Sis, listen, if you have ever experienced or are currently experiencing any type of mental illness, please reach out for support. Get a therapist and take your power back! The enemy wants to take our minds. The Bible says in Romans 12:2, "And be not conformed to this world: but be ye transformed by the renewing of your mind, that ye may prove what is that good, and acceptable, and perfect, will of God." Which means we should also meditate on the word of God daily, and allow His words, His thoughts, and His promises to us to shift our perspective.

I know it's hard sometimes, and we don't understand why God allowed us to go through what we went through but Sis,

YOU MADE IT! I MADE IT! WE MADE IT!

The trauma didn't kill us, the anger won't keep us, and the pain we endured doesn't define us. You can do this, Sis! Trust me, I've been there, and through everything I shared in this chapter, the common factors were me, God, and a determination to not allow the obstacles I faced to keep me down.

I always reminded myself that if I was at my lowest, the only other way to go was up! God had no choice but to show up and show out every single time because that's when He gets the glory!

Whew, Sis! I know that was a lot to process, and I hope it didn't trigger you. So let's take a longer check-in this time!

You good, Sis Mental Health Check-in (Take a 30-minute break)

1. Pause, and take a deep breath

2. You good, Sis? (Ask yourself, am I ok? Do I need a break?) If so, put the book down and come back to it.

3. What did this chapter bring up for you?

4. Were you triggered? If so, let's explore it. Grab your journal, your favorite pen, get your blanket and let's write. Write what you felt; cry, release, and replace all negative beliefs with positive beliefs.

5. If you are currently in a domestic violence relationship and need assistance. Call the domestic violence hotline.

Hotline Numbers

800.799.SAFE (7233)-Domestic Violence National Hotline

1-800-273-8255- National suicide prevention line

Chapter 5

Resilience

*M*ommy, are we going to sleep in the car tonight?

"I don't know, baby. I hope not," I said to my 9-year-old at the time while sitting in the backseat of the white Camry rental car.

We had just pulled into an empty lot next to Chick-fil-a. It crushed me to say that to her, and I felt so helpless, abandoned, and angry all at the same time.

God, I know I heard you tell me to move to Dallas. I know I'm supposed to be here, so what is happening? What did I do wrong? I didn't understand what was happening. *I was finally obedient to what you had been telling me to do for 3 years!! I was obedient to you, Lord, so why am I still struggling? Why aren't things going as planned?*

The real question was, "Sis were you obedient when He told you to? Or did you move on your terms and expect God to act on your plans?"

My Journey to Dallas

The first time I heard the Lord tell me to move to Dallas was in 2011 while in a domestic violence relationship with my ex (my first love/abuser). We were living together with my three children, and after one of our arguments, I heard GOD say it clear as day while standing in the kitchen of our 2-bedroom apartment. "Move to Dallas."

I paused and tried to act as if I didn't hear Him because I knew my ex would not want to go with me. His family was here in Houston. So, what did I do? Yep, I ignored God's voice the first time in 2011.

Every year after that, I heard the Lord tell me to move to Dallas for three years straight, and I ignored Him each time. I made a tradition that the girls and I would spend our New Year in Dallas. No matter what, we would always open our New Year at the Potter's house with our Bishop, T.D Jakes. We celebrated with our family and friends, and it was the highlight of my year. Sometimes I couldn't wait to leave my situation and go release some of what I was feeling. This was my favorite time of year!

"Move to Dallas." There He goes again.

I didn't, but in 2012 I joined the GLL (God's Leading Lady) Hybrid program. I drove up to Dallas every other weekend for months. Throughout every lesson, I was learning about myself, and I was ignoring God's voice saying, "Come to me, daughter. I have provided a way of escape for you. You don't have to stay in a toxic relationship. I am here for you; I want more for you, but you have to trust Me."

The last time I heard God tell me to move to Dallas was in 2013. It was during a fight that me and my ex were having in the restroom. I don't recall a lot of what happened that night. However, I do remember laying on the bathroom floor and hearing him crying over me. I must've blacked out because he was trying to wake me up. I just laid there because I was so tired of fighting and was just ready to give up. Then I heard God say, "When will you trust Me with your life and be obedient? What about your girls?" Then He reminded me that I had been going through Hell to be who HE called me to be, the generational curse breaker. He said, *"It's time to let this season of your life go."* It was time to move from being a victim and take control of my life.

It's so funny how God will talk to you like you already know what He's talking about because you have been ignoring Him. He's like, l*isten, that's enough, you are built for this! It's time to rise now, even in your pain. I gave you grace while you healed; you cried it out, forgave it, and now it's time to put this situation to use! You didn't go through this for you, and your pain is not in vain!*

So, I began talking about jobs with my best friend and a few family members who lived in Dallas, and I started really "considering" moving.

It took me a year and a half, but I did it. I moved to

Dallas and moved in with my best friend, which didn't work. Then my girls and I moved in with another friend, but that didn't work either. We were left homeless late one night, and I felt alone. I had no choice but to depend on God. He had to strip everything and everyone around me that I depended on so I could rely on Him. Everything and everyone who was "safe," familiar, and comfortable He shifted. God created a space for Him and me to build a deeper relationship, just the two of us—no distractions. Yes, He told me to move to Dallas, but when I got there, I was leading the way, asking God to rubber-stamp it. I wasn't consistent in keeping Him first, seeking His face with every decision I made, but I know that our God is a jealous God.

From that moment on, I didn't make one move without praying and fasting first. It was the only thing that helped me to navigate through this battle and walk in my purpose. I was at the feet of Jesus every night because this was one of the lowest points in my life, and I could ONLY call on Jesus. He knew what I needed when my tears hit the steering wheel the first night we slept in a rental car. I didn't have gas money to make it to a hotel, the girl's school, or work, so we slept in the car that night. While they slept, I watched over them; I couldn't sleep at all.

The next morning, we drove to our favorite gas station, QT, cleaned ourselves up, and I dropped them off at school. It was as if nothing different had happened. I wasn't panicked or filled with anxiety at all. I was just in survival mode, which I operated in throughout my entire life, especially when I became a mother. I had to make it happen at all costs. No matter what, at the end of the day, everything fell on God and me. Thankfully, I got paid the next day and could make it to my godmother's house, who was furious we had slept in the car and told me not to do that again. I needed to be careful. I was always welcome there, but I needed to be somewhere safe with my daughters and also get the help and resources we so desperately needed.

The year 2015 was particularly challenging for me. I experienced great losses, betrayals, and hurt. We had to move from three different places for several reasons, and we had only been in Dallas for a few months. Everywhere we went, we were eventually left homeless. I didn't understand what I was doing wrong. I finally went to my godmother and told her everything that was happening. We started talking about how the move and leaving the domestic violence relationship affected the kids and me. We had a few altercations with my ex that ultimately left us exposed and no longer safe to be around my family and friends. Although she wanted to help me, she recommended going to a shelter to be safe and get the resources to help us start over. I fought the idea hard; I was not ready for that, but I knew it was the best decision.

THE SHELTER

While sitting in the driveway of my godmother's house, I made the call to shelter. I was terrified and angry. I felt completely misunderstood. I knew this was the best and safest option for my daughters and me. I started to Google shelters. I spoke to five different organizations, but only two had space. One said they didn't have room for all of us, but the second, Safe Haven, said they would take us, but it had to be the following day. It was almost New Year's Day, and the sweet lady on the phone said I had to get in before the holiday. Safe Haven was normally packed on holidays. My heart and head were in two places. I wanted to be home with my family in Houston, getting ready to celebrate my daughter's birthday. I also wanted to be in Dallas, where God told me to move and not have to feel the rollercoaster of emotions during this transition. I was tired of repeating my story and reliving my trauma over and over, but this was just the beginning. I had no idea my life would change with one decision to be obedient, not only to what God told me to do but doing it through fear.

On my daughter, Chloe's birthday, December 30, 2015, I made one of the hardest decisions in my life. My daughters and I moved into a domestic violence shelter in Fort Worth, Texas. This was tough for me. We could bring only one week's worth of clothing, one stuffed animal or toy, and a few other items. They provided a lot of resources and basic necessities. It was a bittersweet day for me, but I wanted to make sure she enjoyed herself because we are big on birthdays in my family. So, we had a small celebration at Chuck E Cheese, and then we had her favorite pizza, cake, and ice cream.

Our check-in time was at 7pm. Although I was not ready for this, I had to do it. I couldn't believe this was how

Chloe's birthday would end. I was an emotional wreck all day, but of course, as moms, we can sometimes cover up very well. I was smiling through the pain; no one could tell I was not okay because I put on my superwoman cape, laughed, and played with my baby girl the entire day before we had to go.

We were able to keep all the rest of our clothes and other items stored at my godmother's house, and we just changed out every week. God sent my godmother to help me process through all of this, and I couldn't have done it without her. She went above and beyond to help us, including praying and covering us with the word. I am forever grateful for her.

When we got to the shelter, I started thinking and overthinking as I always do in any stressful situation. My anxiety was through the roof! Millions of questions flooded my head. *What am I doing here? Is this really our new reality?* Our new journey had begun, and I had no idea what to expect. I felt like it wasn't real. I was in extreme mama bear mode, protecting my cubs because I didn't trust anyone! I had to make sure they felt safe and comfortable at the same time. Safe Haven blessed us to have an entire room to ourselves with four beds. It was clean with care packages on each bed and a nice note welcoming us.

The kids picked out their beds, and we began to unpack. Since we would be here for the next few months or so, I wanted to make it our own, make it feel and look like a home as much as possible. I went to Walgreens and made each one of us a collage with my mom, their grandparents, and whoever else they wanted on it, printed the pictures out, and hung them over each bed. We prayed and had devotion every night together. We played games in the middle of the floor sometimes for family night. I tried to bring a sense of normalcy to this tough situation. This was very tough for me as a mother. I was extremely uncomfortable and unsure what would happen next, but I continued to trust God through this storm.

The face of Resilience

As I think about the idea of what resilience looks like, how to recognize it, and how to build it, a few things come to mind to help you become more resilient.

- Create a belief in your ability to cope. You can choose what you believe.

- Stay connected with those who support you.

- Talk about what you're going through to a coach, therapist, or other professional.

- Be helpful to others and allow others to help you.

- Focus on what's positive in your life.

- Work on self-awareness, mindfulness, self-care, positive relationship, and purpose.

Resilience is already on the inside of you; all you have to do is activate it! Psychologists define resilience as *the process of adapting well in the face of adversity, trauma, tragedy, threats, or significant sources of stress such as family and relationship problems, serious health problems, or and financial stressors.*

Resilience is my second superpower, and I love it!

REJECTION AND RESILIENCE

As a child, family gatherings and our monthly family prayer calls were moments I looked forward to because I loved spending time with my family. I would see my father at almost every family function, but we didn't have a relationship. It was very uncomfortable to feel that rejection over and over again. We would speak and mingle with the family, but we really didn't talk outside of that. I felt like I was being rejected and slapped in my face every time I saw him, and although I could reach out, hug him, and talk to him, it didn't seem to make it better. At one point, it was like neither one of us wanted to be rejected, so we did not attempt to work on our relationship. Based on our adult relationship and conversations we've had, I choose to believe that my father wanted to have a better relationship with me as a child but didn't know how. He did the best he could with what he had.

You are probably wondering why I am mentioning rejection while talking about resilience. They definitely have a relationship and work hand-in-hand. I didn't recognize it at the time, but while feeling the rejection from my dad, exes, and friendships, I was also building resilience to manage the rejection in other areas of my life. I didn't always handle rejection or hurt without anger until I learned and healed from it.

When you build resilience, you can literally bounce

back from anything life throws at you. Your viewpoint of rejection and offense shifts as you build resilience. Because of our fears and expectations, people with rejection sensitivity tend to misinterpret, distort, and overreact to what other people say and do. They may even respond with hurt and anger. Social rejection increases anger, anxiety, depression, jealousy, and sadness. It reduces performance on difficult intellectual tasks and can also contribute to aggression and poor impulse control.

COPING WITH REJECTION

Acknowledge your emotions-

Rather than suppress, ignore, or deny the pain, we must acknowledge our emotions. We have to admit when we are embarrassed, sad, disappointed, or discouraged. Have confidence in your ability to deal with uncomfortable emotions head-on, which is essential to coping with discomfort in a healthy manner.

Whether you are being rejected by a family member or losing a job, trying to minimize the pain by convincing yourself or someone else it was "no big deal' will only prolong your pain. The best way to deal with uncomfortable emotions is to face them head-on.

Look at rejection as evidence you are **DOING SOMETHING RIGHT!**-

We have to understand rejection serves as proof that you are living life to the fullest. You can also expect to be rejected sometimes. Don't be afraid to go for it, even when you suspect it may be a long shot. You never know what God can do!

If you never get rejected, you may be living too far inside your comfort zone. You can't be sure you're pushing yourself to your limits until you get turned down every now and then. When you get rejected for a project, passed up for a job, or turned down by a friend, you'll know you're putting yourself out there.

Give yourself grace and compassion-

Rather than think, "You're so stupid for thinking you could do that," give yourself some compassion. Respond to negative self-talk with a kinder tone, use some of your favorite affirmations to love yourself at the moment.

Whether you got dumped by your long-term love or blindsided by a recent firing, beating yourself up will only keep you down. Speak to yourself like a trusted friend. You have to be a trusted friend to yourself first. You come first in any situation.

Refuse to let rejection define you-

When you are stronger mentally, you don't make sweeping generalizations when you are rejected. If one company turns you down for a job, rejection will tell you that you are incompetent. Or, if you get rejected by a single love interest, you will conclude you're unlovable, and nobody wants you.

You must keep rejection in perspective by asking yourself, "What did I gain from this?" so you can learn from rejection; rather than simply tolerating the pain. You have the power to turn it into an opportunity for self-growth. With each rejection, you gain the opportunity to grow stronger and become better! I changed the narrative in my life through my mindset and how I perceived pain, hurt, or even correction. You can do this also, Sis!

YOU GOOD, SIS MENTAL HEALTH CHECK-IN (TAKE A 15−20-MINUTE BREAK)

1. Pause, and take a deep breath

2. You good, Sis? (Ask yourself, am I ok? Do I need a break?) If so, put the book down and come back to it.

3. What did this chapter bring up for you?

4. Were you triggered? If so, let's explore it. Grab your journal, your favorite pen, get your blanket and let's write. Write what you felt; cry, release, and replace all negative beliefs with positive beliefs.

Chapter 6

The Making of a CEO

My earliest memory growing up of wanting to be an entrepreneur was in the third grade. I met a Black woman who owned a limousine company on the north side of Houston. I don't remember exactly why we needed a limo at the time. Still, I had never seen a Black Female Entrepreneur. She was very sweet and helped me to visualize and see that my dream was possible and attainable. I was so inspired by her because I always wanted to own a limousine company *and* a beauty brand. She made being a Black female entrepreneur look easy.

While my sister and I lived with my daddy during middle school, he started his own tax business. I remember when he took us to see the building where his business was located. As we walked up the stairs to the front door, I remember thinking, *wow, my daddy has his own business.* I was so happy for him and proud of him; I must say I was intrigued and wanted to know how I could have this for my life. He worked a job and ran his business. He even refereed sometimes. My dad showed me what it took to run a business and maintain life. He had a lot of ambition and drive. I watched my father be consistent in his business and sacrifice so much so we could have. I watched him in the role of a Black Entrepreneur with employees and be a leader to many people. He was my first real experience with entrepreneurship.

I would be at his tax office, not necessarily working but watching him work. Some nights, I just wanted to go home and enjoy being a teenager. Often, I watched him sacrifice sleep and time, and I'm sure he wanted some personal things also. He worked well after the clients and employees had gone home. My dad constantly talked to my sister and me about tithing, saving, and spending. Most of the conversations weren't about spending, though. He reminded us to always give God his 10% first and save as much as we could. He was very intentional about his spending (My daddy is very frugal). So, I had to learn that too! (I'm still working on it, though). Entrepreneurship is in my bloodline; my paternal grandmother owned two-day care centers. I am excited and honored to pass the legacy on to my daughters. Camille already has her own organizing business that she started at 13 years old. Cayleigh, Chloe, my niece Journey, and even my 2-year-old Aundrea all work for me. The best way to teach the next generation is by letting them actually see me running my business. I repeat what my father did to me, which was to show me, not just tell me.

Bold Lips Revolution Cosmetics was born in the season of my life where I was hurting and wanted to help other hurting women. I wanted to show my children that even during the lowest point in your life, you could still help others grow and heal.

When I first moved to Dallas, I didn't know what was coming next or what I should do next. I was nervous, anxious, and excited all at the same time. My friend and I started developing a plan for how my girls and I could build our lives there.

One day she and I talked about what faith looked like and how I needed to completely surrender to God's will for my life, and I chose to completely surrender to God's will; I started fasting, praying, and seeking Him. I started working at a beauty supply store while looking for other jobs. I have always been an entrepreneur at heart and didn't care to "work for other people."

LIPS: My Money Maker

I wanted to do my own thing. So, I thought about my long-term goal of owning my own business. I wanted to start a lip gloss line that empowered young girls who struggled with low self-esteem by showing them how to love themselves fully. Throughout elementary school to eighth grade, I hated my lips. The boys in school always made fun of them, so I would never wear anything bolder than clear lip gloss, although I would wear a lot of it. I didn't want to really "draw attention" to my lips. There was this secret love for them, but I didn't fully embrace them.

While in high school, I told my mom I wanted to be a model because I loved taking pictures. She took me to Page Parkes, one of the top modeling agencies in Houston. The nice lady we met with immediately complimented me on my lips.

"You are beautiful. Are you guys Nigerian?"

I chuckled, "No ma'am, just Black." and we all laughed.

She invited us to have a seat, then said, "I'm sorry, I just love your high cheekbones and your beautiful full lips. So, I assumed you were African."

"Thank you, but I don't like them. My lips are just too big."

"Oh, honey!" she said, shocked, "people pay thousands of dollars for your bottom lip alone! You have to embrace what you have naturally."

I started smiling, "Ok, thank you!"

"You are a little short for fashion, but I could definitely see you doing commercial print modeling. We need more people that look like you."

Although, this was not my first time hearing my lips were beautiful because my parents and family always told me that. I thought, well, you're my family, so you're supposed to say that. We all have the full "Cullins" lips. But to hear it from someone on the outside was refreshing.

She influenced me to change my perspective about my lips, and I began to embrace my insecurities, one by one. As I got older, I started wearing bold colors on my lips, making me feel much better about myself. As women, especially mothers, we have that one insecurity that stands out the most: we wish to just make it disappear.

Shapewear is the magic we all love and need in our lives, just for the extra comfort, of course. I know y'all can agree with me. But I don't care how much we try to hide or cover up that insecurity; it doesn't just disappear. So, I decided to embrace my "Big Lips" by wearing a bold color on them and embracing the thing I once perceived as a bad thing about myself.

By my acceptance, I would also empower other women to embrace their insecurities, rediscover their power through positive affirmations and build their confidence to walk boldly in what God has already placed inside of them.

Through counseling, I learned that my insecurities since childhood affected certain parts of my domestic violence relationship and relationships period. I lacked confidence in many different areas of my life, and I knew other women were dealing with similar experiences.

After fasting and praying for 30 days in November 2015, I heard God say, "Start your lipstick line." I tried to ignore what I heard because I didn't think it was possible or the right time to start a business. I heard Him say it again, and I told my friends what the Lord spoke to me, and they said, "Ok, let's do it!" We support you. After researching "How to start a cosmetic line" on YouTube, we went to the store and bought all the ingredients to make lipstick with "crayons." We literally were mixing crayons in the kitchen. We also started working on sketches for my logo.

The Lord gave me the name, *Bold Lips Revolution,* to change the negative perception of bold lip colors and "Big" lips. He showed me the colors I should release first, the names, and the brand colors. I followed everything to the exact picture He showed me. I didn't make any decisions without praying and seeking God first.

When I went into the shelter, I put BLR on hold to focus on my children and this life-changing experience. I couldn't concentrate on anything else but safety for us.

On January 2nd, 2016, just a few short days of being in the shelter, while my children were in school, I sat in my room, listening to my worship music and journaling. I began asking God why He called me to Dallas, only for us to end up in a shelter. *I had a ton of family in Houston; I can just go back,* I said! *I don't want to be here...* I was crying out to God every day! Praising and worshipping Him even though I didn't understand what was going on.

I felt like Moses in the wilderness begging to hear God's voice for direction. I needed Him to comfort our hearts. I kept hearing Him say, "Continue being obedient; trust me. I will see you through this." Whenever I heard Him speak to me concerning the business, I started making sure that I wrote it all down. It's amazing what happens when God speaks and starts downloading. I learned to let Him take the lead, and I wrote down what I heard. Sometimes all God wants us to do is trust Him and surrender to His will.

God downloaded so much into me that day. He reminded me what my life would be like if I just followed His lead. Obedience is better than sacrifice, and I am so glad I was obedient. He said, "Give a portion of the proceeds back to the women coming behind you. You are called to those women. This is so much bigger than you." I said, "Lord, this is too much right now. I don't even know where to start. I don't want to bleed on other people." I didn't feel "qualified" to serve anyone else.

I would always say, "I don't deserve this, Lord, I'm not worthy." I couldn't understand why He would choose me. Then I got up from the floor and said, "Lord, now? I can't do this; this is too painful for me to process."

He said, "You can do this. I have a plan for you. I have never left you, and I never will. You didn't go through this for nothing. Women's lives will be changed." As I walked out of the doors of the shelter to get the girls from the transportation service, I heard it again, "Donate a portion of your proceeds to survivors of domestic violence."

For a few days, I pondered on this; it was all I could think about. I couldn't talk to anybody about it but my godmother. Even then, I didn't really know what this meant. *I heard what you said, Lord, but this just doesn't make sense to me. I can barely provide for my children, and You want me to purchase products and start a business?* I was so confused but also interested in seeing how He would bring me out of this.

I was at one of the lowest points in my life, so I knew the only other way was up from here. I felt like I reached my hand up to God, and He pulled me up. I am eternally grateful to serve a God that wants to see His children prosper. Just trust Him through the process.

It was very hard for me to accept, but I had to continue to do what God had called me to do even while I was hurting and in pain. I didn't understand how I was going to do any of this.

BLR: Bold Lips Revolution

The next week my friend introduced me to a woman who had her own cosmetics line, who was willing to help me get started with my products. A family friend helped me create my website and set up my business legally. We were official! I was excited and ready to get started! I worked at the Mattel warehouse in Fort Worth during the day. So, I worked on my business in the evenings after picking up my children from daycare, feeding them, and putting them to bed. I was also trying to find somewhere for my children and me to live once we left the shelter.

This was a journey for me. It was not easy, but I kept being obedient. I kept praying and fasting in the Shelter. I allowed the pain I was feeling to fuel my passion for helping women. I had just experienced a lot of losses in friendships and relationships. I was heartbroken, lonely, and depressed sometimes. I definitely could have chosen to give up. I had plenty of reasons to say *this is too much to deal with right now. I'm going home to Houston!*

There were a number of reasons I could have used what I was going through as an excuse to go home to my family, but I knew that God would see me through because He always does. I know my life would not be where it is today had I not been patient through the process; even when it got really bad, I always trusted God's plan for my life. I trusted the vision He had for me. I was determined to live out the scripture, "Obedience is better than sacrifice." Every single day, I chose to be obedient because the sacrifice was never worth the disobedience.

I trusted God through my car repossession right after arriving in Dallas, being homeless with my daughters, living in hotels and sleeping in a rental car, and ultimately birthing my dream while living in a domestic violence shelter. I knew God would guide my footsteps as I followed His voice. The shelter provided us with countless resources, therapy, housing, etc. So, I didn't have to spend any money on things we needed, except for toiletries.

In March of 2016, I got promoted to supervisor at Mattel and began to save money for my business. Shortly after that, we got approved through a transitional housing program that was fully furnished with everything we needed; Clothing vouchers for myself and the kids and gas gift cards. God provided!

While in one of our mandatory weekly group sessions, a few ladies from the church that was connected to the shelter would come to encourage us and bring activities. They mentioned a financial education course their church offered. I was immediately interested and signed up. I wanted to be intentional with my spending and saving. I was reminded of what my father said when talking to us about the importance of budgeting and finance. I learned about budgeting and how to manage my money the way God intended.

Faith and Finances were held every Thursday. They provided childcare and dinner, which was so helpful for me to be a single mom and still work on my business. The girls enjoyed going every week also. Having their support had a major impact on how I handled my finances, and I was able to pick them up from school and go straight to class.

My favorite couple from the church, Ron and Marilyn Holland went out of their way to help us on numerous occasions with my car breaking down, getting resources, and sometimes just having dinner together as a family. They helped me comb through my personal finances and create a budget for my business and personal finances. We had homework; they held us accountable and supported us through the entire course. I was excited about the tools helping me build generational wealth.

In April of 2016, I used my tax refund to purchase my first order of products and scheduled my first photoshoot! I was so excited; I could hardly think straight some nights. I had so many ideas and plans. Things were happening fast that sometimes it didn't feel like I was living in a transitional living home. I definitely didn't look like what I had been through. God is faithful even through the pain and the process of trying to pursue your purpose.

My caseworker was extremely nice and always encouraged me to keep going. She reminded me to tell my story and be authentic. She supported me and always told me how proud of me she was. I was grateful for the genuine support of the people around me.

God was already showing out, but He was just getting started. In May 2016, our products debuted in Miami Fashion Week and in October New York Fashion Week with Robin LULU before officially launching. This was huge! I am forever grateful for the exposure God has allowed.

Shortly after we launched, I was invited to a benefit dinner hosted by Safe Haven Shelter of Tarrant County. I was able to bring my business cards and network with other people. I met an amazing woman, my new friend, Hannah. I walked up to her and handed her my business card, and we began talking about her dress matching my lipstick. We talked about my story, my heart, and the passion behind the lipstick line. I had no idea what she did for a living. I thought she was just someone I was networking with. After talking for several minutes, she said she was a reporter for WFAA news in Dallas and would love to do a story on my journey. I was shocked and a little nervous about this because I didn't know what to expect. I honestly thought it wasn't real until she contacted me about a time to come and record the segment. I couldn't believe I was going to be on TV! *What should I say? What do I wear?* I had so many questions, but I was so excited about this opportunity.

The segment aired and went viral. I started getting speaking engagements in Houston, Dallas, and the surrounding areas. People were inspired by my story and wanted me to inspire others. As I reflect on that time in my life, I couldn't understand why people wanted to hear my story. What was so good about what I went through? Did my story have that much value that other people wanted to hear? From the outside looking in, it may look like, *wow, she's so strong and powerful to do something from such a low place in her life.* I struggled because I was still hurting and didn't feel "qualified" to be in this position.

I started going to therapy while in the shelter, and I still go to this day. Whenever I would talk to my therapist about what I was going through, she would ask me probing questions. Those questions helped me think about why I viewed myself as unworthy for people to hear my story. Why was I concerned that my story wasn't good enough to help somebody else? I started to see my purpose in life as greater than my own. I wasn't in control; God is and always will be. He is the reason I can share my story with the world. I stopped self-sabotaging and started believing God's promises in my life.

I channeled all of that energy and lessons I was learning into building BLR. I constantly reminded myself that if my story touches one person, everything I went through was worth it! I took notes, pictures, and videos to remember how I felt in those moments to effectively help other survivors who wanted to start their own business after leaving an abusive relationship. I wanted to show other women it's possible to build generational wealth for their families no matter the situation.

BLR Beauty is an Empowerment Cosmetics brand. Not only does our make-up enhance your beauty, but it also empowers women to be the strong, bold females they were destined to be. Each product name represents the characteristics that symbolize the strength of women because they should be praised and reminded of how BOLD and REVOLUTIONARY they are. We empower women to embrace their insecurities and wear confidence boldly.

To the business owner, entrepreneur, or aspiring entrepreneur who wants to start their business and are afraid, you good, Sis! You can do this! I did it, and I am NO different than you. To the abuse survivor struggling to decide if she wants to go back to the abusive relationship, you good, Sis! You have support to help you get through this. You are not alone. Reach out to your support system, and of course, call on the Battle Buddies Tribe for encouragement when you feel like you can't do it. Remember who you are, *whose* you are and what you deserve!

You good, Sis! You have the power to shift your mindset and perspective around your current situation and your future. Trust yourself and show up for yourself!

YOU GOOD, SIS MENTAL HEALTH CHECK-IN (TAKE A 15−20-MINUTE BREAK)

1. Pause, and take a deep breath

2. You good, Sis? (Ask yourself, am I ok? Do I need a break?) If so, put the book down and come back to it.

3. What did this chapter bring up for you?

4. Were you triggered? If so, let's explore it. Grab your journal, your favorite pen, get your blanket and let's write. Write what you felt; cry, release, and replace all negative beliefs with positive beliefs.

Chapter 7

Your Personalized Mental Health Check-In

People have often asked me how I started my cosmetics line while living in a domestic violence shelter. They would ask what my mental space looked like during that time to process what I was going through, working at a job, with three daughters, and a full-time student? One recurring question was, "How were you able to focus on building a business?"

Honestly, Sis, I felt like I was on autopilot and in survivor mode. I wasn't really living in the moment, and sometimes, I was going through the motions. Yes, I was still trusting God, praying, and fasting, but I had moments where I felt like giving up and not wanting to do anything because it got overwhelming.

As previously mentioned, a few weeks after we got to the shelter, the girls and I started individual and group counseling. Sometimes it was very hard to push through the pain, loss, and constant rejection I felt having to process the last few years of my life, but I felt like I had to show up for them. I had to be strong for them and lead by example. If they were willing to go to play therapy every week and talk to their therapist, I could make myself get the most out of it even when I didn't want to.

My therapist was the sweetest person you will ever meet; very compassionate and caring yet straight to the point. She helped me rediscover who I was as a person, what triggered me, and how my life experiences affected me. We often talked about self-care and making sure it was a priority. I never really enjoyed resting because I would associate rest or sleep with feelings of being lazy. So, it was hard to rest even when I knew I needed to. She reminded me I couldn't care for my children if I didn't care for myself and how I couldn't give from an empty cup. She encouraged me to take moments for myself and get to know Monet again.

I noticed a lot of the times I was angry, anxious, or on edge about something. I was triggered by my childhood and the abusive relationship often. I was always tired, and not just physically but mentally and emotionally drained. So, I decided to intentionally monitor who and what I allowed to be deposited into my spirit. I paid attention to how I felt after having a conversation with certain people and acted accordingly. That meant I didn't share certain information with particular people because of the continued negative response or perspective. Or if the person was draining more than it was a healthy two-way exchange of support. I have to protect my peace at all costs. We have to be mindful of what we watch, what we listen to, and who we take counsel or advice from. Protecting your ear and eyes have to be a top priority. After I went to the shelter, I vowed, no one would take me back to the place of negativity and toxicity. One thing to remember, to grow, you must be stretched.

Google defines stretching as being capable of being made longer or wider WITHOUT tearing or breaking. That says to me, no matter how much pressure is put on me, and no matter the amount of stress or how long it takes, I will not and cannot break. You good, Sis, they can't break you, and you will grow from this. You are stronger than you think. Philippians 4:13 says, " I can do all things through Christ who strengthens me. So we don't rely on your own strength, if we fully surrender to God and let Him carry us.

Self-Sabotage

Trauma responses show up in different ways. Hurt people not only hurt people, but they hurt themselves because they can't hurt the ones that hurt them. This is all about self-sabotaging. We have desires and wants, and the vision, but we still self-sabotage. We don't think we deserve it based on what man says and what our experiences have taught us. God will tell what will happen, but the next thought is me talking myself out of it because it sounds too good to be true. I am not the only one. We all do this. God would show me visions and speak to me through dreams. I would even get prophecies that confirmed what he showed, but I struggled to believe it and walking it.

Self-sabotage is real. My first time hearing about it was in transitional living after leaving the domestic violence shelter. The caseworker said she believed I was self-sabotaging, based on our weekly meetings and consistently hearing my view of everything around me. She asked, "Why don't you think you deserve all the good things coming your way?" I was intrigued. This was an aha moment. I wanted to know more; I wanted to understand the layers of the trauma I had experienced since childhood. I did things impulsively and made so many poor decisions. Another way I self-sabotaged was by not dealing with problems until they get so big that you are forced to deal with them.

Self-sabotage can have many causes, but the end result is that you get off track, mess up relationships, don't get things done, or don't perform as well as you would like. All of this can lead to feeling bad about yourself and expecting to fail, which leads to more self-sabotage to avoid facing failure head-on, which perpetuates the cycle.

Allowing myself to make these poor decisions affected the entire trajectory of my life. If we would get rid of the notion that we are undeserving, that it's too good to be true, that God didn't mean that for me, we could easily take power and control of our lives.

As you can probably imagine, after going to jail a few times, I have a criminal background that has affected me in every area of my life. I struggled with getting an apartment in my name, getting and keeping a decent job. I couldn't get anything in my name, I mean, I was really struggling, but it's because of my self-sabotaging behaviors, poor choices, and lack of trust in God. I had to get to a place where I could hear God clearly. I needed to know without a shadow of a doubt that it was His voice telling me what to do and His spirit guiding me on how to do it.

Whew, Sis! I'm so glad I recognized those behaviors and started to shift my mindset. I TRUSTED GOD even more than changing my thoughts. Imagine trying to find a nice neighborhood for you and your girls to live in where they will get an exceptional education, and it's affordable.

You find the perfect apartment. YOU LOVE IT, but then the self-sabotaging thoughts tell you, "You know they will reject you when they run your background." But you apply anyway, pay the fee (sometimes it was my very last), and then PRAY to God that they will somehow approve you. I remember working with a realtor to help me find a person with a house to rent that would rent to me. Trying to get into an apartment was out of the question. I had family and friends that put apartments in their name for me a few times, but they were only 1-year leases. So, every year towards the end of the lease, I would get extreme anxiety about the entire situation. I hated to hear the words, "Hi Ms. Cullins, you qualify financially, and we would love to have you, but your background won't allow us to accept you."

The constant rejection made me feel alone and helpless. But I knew God had a purpose for my pain. Even though I made those poor decisions, God would still get the glory out of this situation. So, I trusted God with my pain and chose to be vulnerable and bold enough to speak my own truth. God fueled my superpower of being transparent and honest about my story, and He told me to give him the rest. Some nights before and after applying, I would blast worship music and cry out to God for Him to take control.

So, I began looking for houses in the areas God told me to from that moment on! They were always in good neighborhoods, good school districts, and safe for my daughters and me. From that day forward, I prayed about each property I saw before applying because I didn't want to move somewhere that's not in the will of God for my life. I had fully surrendered to His will in this area. I began to walk into the offices to apply for a house with such boldness and authority. Every time I applied, I provided them with a letter explaining what they would find on my background, what happened and how I had changed. I explained I was a single mom of three girls and a full-time student trying to change my life and create a better legacy for my daughters. I prayed over it and turned it in. I thanked them for their time even if they didn't approve of me.

That letter helped me get into three places in my name! God worked it out every single time! The first house I moved into was a 3-bedroom 2 bath home. The landlord took $50 off the rent every month to help me when she realized I was in school, using my school refund to support us. One property saw me trying and wanted to help me, so they approved and renewed my lease for another year. The third property was the transitional living in Dallas after leaving the shelter. I submitted the same letter to them, and they approved me as well. I am so grateful for this experience because it has taught me how to be grateful for everything God gives you. Don't take anything for granted. God is always there, I promise. He sent His angels to remind me He is always in control; He always sends you signs. You just have to pay attention to them.

So, to the single mother struggling to make ends meet, the mother with a criminal background, you good Sis, God will provide. Trust His will for your life and lean not unto your own understanding.

LET'S TALK BOUNDARIES

I had to learn to create healthy boundaries...boundaries... boundaries.

When I heard the boundaries, I associated negative thoughts and negative connotations, and I didn't see it as a good thing. Boundaries to me initially were a guard and a way to keep people out, which I didn't like to do because I am a people pleaser. However, protecting my mind, ear, and eye gates and creating healthy boundaries were crucial and necessary for real transformation and growth.

Imagine driving down a street, and someone tried to swerve into your lane. There is a median to stop people from entering your lane to hurt and crash into you. Although some accidents happen, the barrier was there to prevent the accident from happening.

Boundaries help you maintain peace. It teaches people how to treat you by giving them a blueprint of what you will and won't accept. You are in control of protecting your space and peace. You choose your boundaries and must hold people accountable to them. One of the biggest misconceptions about boundaries is that we expect people to respect and adhere to the boundary without accountability. You can't create a boundary, expect people to respect it, and not hold them accountable when they don't. This gives you peace, so you show them what the consequences of breaking a boundary look like. People will hurt and misuse you as long as you allow them to. Choosing me unapologetically has been the best decision in my life, and you can do it too!

So, let's do something a little different with the mental health check for this chapter.

This is your personal *You Good Sis? Daily Mental Health Check-In.*

You can write this down in your favorite journal or in the notes section of your phone. I like to set the alarm at the beginning of the day to remind myself to do these five easy but intentional actions.

1. Prioritize your self-care time EVERY DAY.

Prioritize a time every day to do something that is fulfilling to you. Something that you enjoy. This doesn't involve helping ANYBODY else. This is your time and yours alone. Go for a walk in the park, write in a journal. Treat yourself to a spa day. Love yourself; you deserve it!

2.   Choose a specific time throughout your day to rest.

Be intentional about "restoration." Enjoy your time to pause. I am intentional about my naps every day. It is on my calendar, and I never forget to take it, but it's good to have it in my schedule, so nothing else interferes with it. Hi, my name is Monet, and I love to sleep. But seriously, rest could be filling up your cup with the word of God and worship music. I have a breathing meditation app I use for 10 min out of my day to stop, pause, breath, and calm my mind.

3.   Forgive and forget yesterday's troubles and embrace today.

We can't move forward with the things of today, carrying the baggage and weight from yesterday. To be fully present today, we must release and forgive yesterday's offenses, hurts, and betrayals. Start by thinking about "what" you are thinking about. Are they negative thoughts from yesterday, last week, last month? Are they positive and motivating? Do I need to forgive and release this? Journal your responses and start noticing when you allow the negative thoughts to take priority over the positive ones. Experts say we produce up to 50,000 thoughts a day, and 70 to 80% of those parts are negative. So, if we bring those negative thoughts into the next day combined with the negative thoughts of the present day, imagine the pressure that weighs on your mental health.

4. **Repeat positive affirmations and Scriptures DAILY to yourself in the mirror.**

Use "I am" statements, and be sure to actually BELIEVE IT when you speak it. Believing is the activation behind words you speak. I am an affirmation girl, and I love sticky notes, so I have different color sticky notes all over my house with positive affirmations on them. When I see them, I am intentional about reading them out loud and believing what I'm reading. I also have a few of my favorite affirmations written on my mirror and my favorite BLR cosmetics lipstick colors. I am literally inundated with affirmations, scriptures, and reminders of what God says about me. Here are a few of my favorites:

I am resilient. I believe in the woman I am becoming. I am fearfully and wonderfully made. I am Enough. I am proud of the woman I am today. I am powerful in all I do and think. I am in control of my destiny. I am a generational curse breaker. I have mental, emotional stability. I am a conqueror through Christ Jesus. I am creating generational wealth for my family. I have the power to control my thoughts. I am confident I can achieve any goal. I am releasing self-judgment and embracing self-love. I am at peace with my past. I am strong and brave. I am letting go of all that no longer serves me. My goal is possible. I am capable of learning new things. My ideas are important and valuable. I do the best that I can every day. I am in control of my life.

5.   Is your Sis GOOD? Are the people around you ok?

Sometimes we forget to check on our strong friends. We assume that because they are always the ones giving and being compassionate and empowering others, they don't need encouragement. We must remember they are some of the main ones who suffer in silence. I was the strong Sis, so I understand firsthand. So, call or text a friend, family member, or coworker and let them know you are here to support them. "*You good, Sis,*" also means we empower, encourage, and uplift the women around us. It's all about community and creating support. So many of us suffer in silence, even with people around us. I encourage you to be kind and caring to others; you never know what they may be dealing with silently. A smile, text, or call can go a long way. Let's normalize giving grace and compassion to others, especially one we think doesn't deserve or need because they appear to be ok.

So, this is me checking on you; you good, Sis?

YOU GOOD, SIS MENTAL HEALTH CHECK-IN (TAKE A 15−20-MINUTE BREAK)

1. Pause, and take a deep breath
2. You good, Sis? (Ask yourself, am I ok? Do I need a break?) If so, put the book down and come back to it.
3. What did this chapter bring up for you?
4. Were you triggered? If so, let's explore it. Grab your journal, your favorite pen, get your blanket

and let's write. Write what you felt; cry, release, and replace all negative beliefs with positive beliefs.

5. Ask yourself, who can I serve today?

Chapter 8

The Forgiven Forgive

～◎◎～

I'll never forget the first time seeing my mother with a black eye and bruises on her face after hearing her and my stepfather argue. I have some very vivid memories, and some are blurred, but my feelings were real. I think I was around seven or eight years old at the time, and I remember it being shortly after their wedding. I was staring at her swollen face, rubbing her back, and feeling the pain while studying her facial expression and gestures. I was on edge. I didn't know what to do or what to say. My mommy was hurting, and I didn't know how to help her.

"Mama, can't we just leave him? Please?" I don't like when the two of you fight." As tears rolled down our faces, we rode to the store. She gently rubbed my face and said, "It's okay, baby, mommy is okay—we're okay. We are married now, and everything is going to be okay."

The belief was implanted in me that even if your husband abuses you, you must work through the issues with him. I understood that it was okay for him to be abusive because he had abandonment issues and anger problems. I believed you had to stay to help him with his issues because that's what love looked like. Eventually, he stopped being physically abusive to my mom. They remained married for a few more years and later divorced. In my mind, it showed me to stick it out with him; eventually, the two of you will figure it out, and the abuse will stop.

This belief stuck with me through my abusive relationship. I thought I could help him process his trauma and vice-versa. We had some really good times and some really bad ones. Although we weren't married yet, I would do what I saw my mom do.

Growing up, and for most of my childhood, I always wondered why she was so frustrated all the time. I could feel the anger coming from her when she 'whipped" us. She spoke to us with such a condescending tone, and I never understood why. The verbal abuse was worse than the physical sometimes, and her tone seemed as if she was annoyed and overwhelmed. It was often chaotic and painful.

You see, I was physically and verbally abused as a child by my mother. CPS was involved a few times. We were taken from our home and lived with my grandparents for a while. This was traumatic and confusing, especially at 7 years old when you don't fully understand. We could visit with my mom, but we couldn't go anywhere with her by ourselves, and that bothered me. I didn't understand why this was happening. I knew she didn't mean to do it because she apologized every single time. So, I was angry at them for taking me from my mom but relieved I wasn't being abused. This shaped my mindset and my entire way of being.

As a teenager, We didn't have the mother-daughter relationship I desired; the abuse continued, and we grew further apart. I'll never forget the bruise on my left inner thigh. I ran my fingers across it and felt the "u shape" of the extension cord. Every time I went to the bathroom and traced it, I relived the trauma again. It seemed like every time I traced it, I pushed it deeper and deeper into my skin. It became a scar and eventually disappeared from my skin but not from my soul. The whipping happened, yet the bruise had a lasting effect. It was a physical representation of the deeper pain that I felt.

When I became a mom, we communicated more. We were more forgiving, and I was able to get a better understanding of my mother. No, everything wasn't perfect, and it took a lot of time and therapy for me to SEE her for who she was and has always been to me.

Forgiving Mom

When you have experienced the abuse, you have these "trauma lenses" on that cause you to see things, people, and experiences in a different light, or should

I say darkness. Trauma lenses are like blinders. They influence your perspective, decision-making, and ability to see things from a healthy and healed perspective. When you can slowly start to remove the lenses from your eyes through therapy, forgiveness, and inner healing, you can shift the trajectory of your life and your relationships with people.

After forgiveness, I was able to see her without the trauma lenses in my adult life. Her strength as a Black woman who survived all she has been through is so inspiring. I learned more about who I am the more I studied her. I began to heal pieces in me I didn't know needed healing.

I'll never forget the time my mother asked for forgiveness for the abuse in my childhood. It was unexpected and completely caught me off guard. It was as if something broke in me, and I was healed at the same time. I felt as if my mommy was holding the little abused girl inside of me, and I just laid in her arms and cried and cried. We healed some things that night, and I'm forever grateful. It takes understanding and, most of all, forgiveness to get to this place. I want other mothers and daughters across the world to begin to reconcile their relationships, heal and move on. We have to protect our wombs and the wombs of our future generations. One mother and daughter at a time...

On the other side of that, I have so many good memories. One that sticks out the most was while I was sleeping, the feeling of oil dripping down my face and her hand on my forehead as she prayed for us in her prayer language. Although I didn't like the oil dripping, her hand on my forehead reminded me she would always cover us. She always covers us, even now. Prayer is her first language, in my opinion. She constantly showed us how a God-fearing woman should live. She isn't perfect, but she led by example by teaching us to have pride in ourselves. She showed us how to pray through her pain with her actively going to prayer revivals at church. She always made jokes or danced around the house to make us laugh, and she is still very protective of us. She always seemed to have it together on the outside. No matter how bad things got or what she was dealing with, she never complained. She always figured it out and pushed through.

I could see her pain and suffering while trying to smile through it all. She was always praying and ministering to others through her pain. She is the true definition of resilience. My mother has been through a lot in her life and never gave up. She sacrificed a lot for us all the time and never said a word about it. She is strong. My mom always made sure we had what we needed and most of what we wanted. Christmas and Birthdays were some of the best moments in our house. We were a little "spoiled." She and my stepdad always made sure we had the parties we wanted and most of the things off our list. We created great memories together as a family that stands out but not as much as the scary ones. I always wondered why it had to be this way.

After having children of my own and experiencing very similar situations as a parent, I was now in her exact shoes with my three daughters. I could feel the pain she felt. I understood why she made certain decisions. I started to piece together the trauma from her childhood and the trauma I experienced, and how it could show up in my children. I realized my mom suffered a lot throughout her childhood. The loss of her mom, abuse in her childhood, and her marriage and then repeating the cycle with us. Often, we have to forgive people because they were victims as well. Some of us need to forgive the abused, broken child within us first to forgive the person who harmed us. I had to have a conversation with myself and say, *give yourself grace, Sis, you were a child, and nothing you did was your fault. You didn't deserve this. You can break this cycle with your children, and you will. But first, you must forgive. Forgive yourself, then release it. I chose to forgive myself for allowing my trauma experiences to dictate how I lived my life. I forgave myself for embracing toxicity and not fully living In my purpose. I feel so forgive myself for self-sabotaging and settling for things that did not start me in for the mistakes that I made along this journey of my life. Forgiving myself helped me to understand forgiveness in a different way. If I could forgive myself, I definitely could forgive those around me who had easily offended me or not intentionally offended me. I begin to embrace forgiveness and pass it out freely.*

I chose to forgive and give her grace once I realized the full impact of the trauma she experienced. Remembering forgiveness is not for the person; it's for me. I needed to release the anger and bitterness. Forgiveness releases the past, people are released, and we are free from the bitterness, guilt, and shame attached to everything we touch in life. The forgiven forgive. The healed heals.

Jesus never would have fulfilled His calling without forgiveness. He asked the Father to forgive the people who offended Him before dying on the cross. We can't fulfill our calling without forgiveness. God gives us forgiveness, and He gives it to us freely. So, why do we make people pay for things that we got for free?

Suppose we don't deal with the root of the unforgiveness. In that case, it attaches itself to every relationship that we have. It will affect the way we think, what we say, and God's destiny for us. We have to deal with the root of bitterness, and we can't have unforgiveness and walk into our destiny. It also keeps us out of environments that God has called us into.

The challenge is that we carry hurt and pain on the inside, and it can give us a license to treat people however we want to treat them. Then your excuse becomes, wait, you don't understand I've just been hurt. Now, my past pain is causing me to mistreat this person in this relationship.

Sis, listen to me when I say this; we don't bleed on people. Especially people that didn't hurt us. Hurt people hurt people, and healed people heal people. Broken people do broken things; healed people do healed things.

You will never have to forgive anybody more than GOD has forgiven you. Think about the wrong you have done in your life. How many times have you asked God for forgiveness? Think about how you felt asking for forgiveness, how you had to humble yourself and pray that God would forgive you. The difference between human reactions and God's reaction to forgiveness is that God will forgive you immediately when you repent. Some people will hold on to unforgiveness for decades, thinking that it is hurting the other person. They are actually re-traumatizing themselves over and over again whenever they think about that memory.

A Daughter's Love – Forgiving Dad

There was nothing you could tell me about my dad. I didn't care what he did. I was always going to defend him. My granny always said I was always with my daddy, even when he went to college. I was right beside him on the weekends. I was a daddy's girl...his firstborn child. So, of course, I was the special one. Or at least that's what I told myself subconsciously, but I didn't regularly feel it. I sought out advice, sometimes financial support to help with my daughters, and even one on one dates. I wanted to know why he couldn't respond to me but chose to respond and have a relationship with everyone else. I wanted to have a genuine relationship with my father, so I attempted to text and call, but I rarely got a response, which caused me to ask these questions, and other family members in my family would say,

"Your daddy was crazy about you when you were little."
"He loves you; you are his firstborn."

Or my all-time favorite, "That's just how he is. He doesn't answer when I call either." Those words didn't do anything but make it worst for my thought process.

Whenever I talked to my granny or others about their perspective of our relationship, how they thought I should approach having a relationship with him as an adult. They always referred to our relationship when I was a child, and it always puzzled me because I didn't feel the close bond they spoke about when I was a child.

My sister is my daddy's twin, and I am my momma's twin. (Literally) They are alike in so many ways, and sometimes I felt as if my mom and I were almost identical. There was a disconnect somewhere in my dad and my relationship, and I didn't know how to handle that as a child. I wanted a closer relationship with my dad so bad. Still, I didn't want to continue to feel the rejection and the feeling of not being enough. I didn't want to hear the excuses or reason why not.

I felt that my decisions as an adult caused him to look at me differently because I was constantly disappointing him. I believe he allowed my sins to cover me, and that's all he saw when he looked at me. I wanted to make my dad proud so much, but it seemed like I just couldn't do it. I chased his approval and validation for years. I continued to go to college while in a domestic violence relationship to get his acceptance and support.

My dad still gives the best hugs in the world. I remember always wanting to feel his hugs, needing his hugs to help me get through whatever I was dealing with at the time. I looked forward to them. I felt so safe in those moments the hug would last. Sometimes it felt like an eternity because I would just pause, breathe, and relax in the security I felt while he held me. I would just take it all in. He would literally squeeze my sister and me until we coughed and then laugh it off with an "Oh sorry, are you okay?" We would both laugh, and I loved those moments growing up. He's the cleanest man on the entire planet, very much disciplined, and has a heart for helping young people. He is a die-hard Cowboy's fan and an Alpha man. I loved being around him. Even though I gave him a run for his money. I was desperately seeking his attention, and he was a single dad trying to do the best that he could.

CPS placed my sister and me with my dad while I was in Middle School, and we were there from 6th to 8th grade. Those were some of the most fun, happy, and confusing times of my life. It was different for all three of us, we had never lived with my Father, and he had gotten full custody of us. So, this was a new journey for us to embark on.

I started meeting new friends, trying to fit in, and acting out. I started being bullied by girls on the bus who made fun of what I was wearing or that my breasts were "too little, "and we would fight. I was always fighting, but I was tired of being abused, and I wasn't gonna let anyone else hurt me. I became extremely rebellious and disobedient. I honestly believe that my behavior got worse as I got older but only because I didn't know how to communicate my emotions effectively.

While my dad was refereeing a game, I invited a boy from the neighborhood over one Friday evening. I was in the 8th grade at the time. We watched one of my favorite shows WWE SmackDown on the big screen TV for about five minutes, and my dad walked in. He looked tired, disappointed, and angry at the same time. I immediately felt remorseful for being disobedient and wished I could take it back. He always made it very clear never to have anyone in his house, and I honestly believe that was the final straw. He sent me back to my mom's house, and I was so hurt and dejected.

This was the first real feeling of rejection from my Father. How could you send me back to a place you rescued me from? He knew what was going on, maybe not everything, but he knew something had happened. He got custody of my sister and me because of the abuse, yet he sent me back. The whipping I got that night has stuck with me more than any other time. She seemed to be whipping her sixteen-year-old self for getting pregnant, and I hadn't ever had sex. It scared me. I had to forgive him for this also. I had to understand that he did the best that he could with what he had. I changed my perspective and saw that my Father was awarded custody of his two girls and cared for us for two years. I imagined what that must've felt like as a single father. I watched the sacrifices he made for us, working hard to make sure we had what we needed.

I learned how to cook on the George Foreman grill for the first time with my dad. He showed us how to make healthy meals such as grilled chicken breasts, green beans, and corn. He was very particular about what he ate and how he took care of his body. I will never forget those experiences, and I will never forget what he instilled in us. I remember waking up at 5 AM every morning before school to have devotion and prayer after getting dressed. My sister and I sometimes would fall asleep while reading our devotional. Still, my Father made us do it every single morning.

I always admired how he was very disciplined and consistent in everything that he did. You could literally judge down to the minute what he was going to be doing in the morning. He hates to be late.

A few months before graduating high school, my dad and I reconciled our relationship. We became closer, but that only lasted a short period. Before I moved to college, we talked about staying focused and remembering what they taught me. Making sure that I keep God first in all that I do. He wanted to make sure that I enjoyed the college experience. He understood that there were certain things that I was never able to do growing up and having such freedom to do it. He begged me not to get pregnant, to break the generational curse off of our bloodline.

"Please finish school first, travel the world, and everything else will come."

I promised him that I would not get pregnant and I would finish school no matter what. When I got to college, he began helping me with my math homework because I absolutely hated math, and he's great with it. We bonded over hard math problems, and we joked about which job I should get working on campus. He taught me how to budget my money and how to find cheap books. A year and a half into college, I got pregnant, and he dropped me again. I was devastated. I felt rejected again and abandoned. I wanted to do everything I could to make sure I graduated and keep that promise. I had to fix this. I had to make my dad proud. I was tired of disappointing him. I was not going to give up; I kept telling myself I could do this.

I will never forget the day I walked across the stage. My family from Houston came down to support me. My dad said he couldn't make it which devastated me. I thought to myself, *you and my daughters are the reason I continued to go forward.* This was the moment where I thought I would get the stamp of approval I needed. And Sis... I got it!

My dad surprised me and came to Dallas for my

graduation. I was sitting with my fellow graduates, and I looked up, and he was walking up the bleachers with my family! I was so excited, anxious, and so happy to see him. I couldn't wait to get my hug! This is the power of forgiveness. If I hadn't begun to forgive him for the things that offended me or what happened to me, I might not have wanted him to be there. Bitterness and anger keep relationships from growing and developing, and we are all forever changing. Be patient, forgive easily, and love harder. My dad and my relationship is not where I want it to be, but we are definitely in a better space than we have ever been.

FORGIVING MY EX, "THE ABUSER."

The abuse, confusion in my childhood, and lack of self-worth led me into an abusive relationship.

I knew this was wrong, but I couldn't see my way out, and my view was obscured and filtered through trauma lenses. Often people who haven't experienced domestic violence don't know what it feels like to be in a situation where you are in love with someone who abuses you. When you've experienced so many different strengths and gains, losses, and wins, conquered so many things together that you don't want to give up on the relationship.

There is a rollercoaster of emotion that you experience during and after a domestic violence relationship. There are a lot of things to unpack. When I talk about experiencing a loss, it's the loss of the relationship. Although it was abusive to me, it was everything that I thought that I needed. It was my safe place. It was my comfort space. The abuse was what I was used to, what was common to me, and a safe space for me.

I learned how to survive while being in that relationship, just as I did as a child. I learned how to decide what I would do and what I would not do to survive in that relationship. The horrible and traumatic experiences of that relationship taught me something else about myself and my pain. You see, to be able to deal with pain, you have to understand it. You have to know its origin. I believe that if you understand the source of the pain, what made you get offended and feel that emotion, then you're able to say, "Okay, this is what happened to me. I can deal with it. I can forgive. I can move on." This understanding helped me forgive my ex.

Once I understood trauma and the source of his trauma, I understood he wasn't just abusive because he wanted to be or just being narcissistic. I knew that he needed help; he was a trauma victim also. If I didn't forgive him, I would end up reliving it and repeating the cycle. I had to let go, I did, and I still am. Forgiveness is a process, and sometimes some things triggered me that I thought I had forgiven and released, but I hadn't. So I am intentional about forgiving those memories and experiences when they come back up.

Before a doctor prescribes any pain medication, he asks about your symptoms or where the pain is. So, he can prescribe the correct medications. We use medicines for many different reasons. Forgiveness is like that; it has the power to heal the pain we feel about the offense. Learning not to be easily offended and realizing that I choose whether I am offended, I no longer take things personally. I receive constructive criticism and the things people say easier than I did before. I no longer hear what people say from a place of attack or offense. I take it at face value and move forward accordingly.

Reading my great-grandmother's book helped me so much. She said that you should forgive almost instantaneously. Dismiss it, and don't let it sit at all. Is this easy? No, but it is necessary for your healing.

The moment you are offended, release it immediately and instantaneously. Otherwise, it will enter into the realm of the subconscious mind and be hidden in this realm which is just as real as the awareness level of your mind, and this could cause trauma to you without you being aware of the cause."

God heals all pains. God is the God of all comfort. God can comfort you in your loss, in your pain. Now, don't get me wrong. **I'm not saying** that you should allow yourself to get comfortable in a domestic violence relationship and just deal with the pain. I am suggesting that you surround yourself with people that can support you, surround yourself with people that are like you, that have experienced what you have experienced.

I don't say this to disregard people that have never experienced domestic violence. However, people who have experienced it, fellow survivors, and fellow advocates can help you through their personal experience and training. Even if you're not able to gather two or three friends, because we know that when the attacker wants to isolate us, often, it's not possible to have support. But I can tell you that your relationship with Christ is your secret weapon. God is the relationship that you rely on. God is the support that you depend on when you feel like you don't have anyone.

A PRAYER OF FORGIVENESS TO BE PRAYED FOR HEALING OF PAST MEMORIES

Almighty Father, in the name of Jesus, I ask your Holy Spirit to bring to my memory conscious or subconscious anyone I need to forgive in Jesus' name.

(Wait quietly in the Holy Spirit, He might show a name, show an incident, show a vision, etc.)

Then pray Almighty Father in the name of Jesus by the acts of my will I choose to forgive_____ (insert the name or names of a person or persons or incidents), I thank you, Father, that I do forgive them and release them to you and receive my forgiveness from you.

Continue to pray this. You will feel cleansed and refreshed. Do it daily until all unforgiveness is gone and past memories cause no more trauma to the mind. Remember, forgiveness is a journey, and when you choose to forgive someone, it doesn't happen immediately, but just make the first step in saying I forgive you even if you don't feel it. Let the Holy Spirit do the rest.

YOU GOOD, SIS MENTAL HEALTH CHECK-IN (TAKE A 15−20-MINUTE BREAK)

1. Pause, and take a deep breath

2. You good, Sis? (Ask yourself, am I ok? Do I need a break?) If so, put the book down and come back to it.

3. What did this chapter bring up for you?

4. Were you triggered? If so, let's explore it. Grab your journal, your favorite pen, get your blanket and let's write. Write what you felt; cry, release, and replace all negative beliefs with positive beliefs.

5. WRITE OUT A LIST OF PEOPLE THAT YOU NEED TO FORGIVE, NO MATTER HOW LONG IT IS, GET IT OUT ON PAPER, AND BEGAN TO FORGIVE EACH

PERSON AND SITUATION ONE BY ONE. PRAY THE
PRAYER AND PASS THIS ON TO YOUR OTHER
FAMILY MEMBERS AND FRIENDS

Bonus Question

What can you do differently in your current situation
that will affect the trajectory of your life? Take your
time and think about this one.

Chapter 9

It's the Inner Healing for me...

I remember being pregnant with my oldest daughter Camille and talking to my great granny about how I was nervous about being a mother. I didn't feel qualified or good enough to be a mother, and I was terrified I would repeat the same cycle as my mom. I wasn't married and didn't have any help from her father. But I wanted to make sure I was "perfect" for her. Especially spiritually, I didn't want to pass those negative spirits to her. I didn't want her to feel the negative emotions and pains that I felt. I'll never forget hearing her soft voice say, "God wouldn't have given you this baby if He didn't think you could handle the weight of carrying it. God has trusted you with this blessing, and you are going to be a great mother."

Whenever we had conversations, she always spoke with such love and grace. One day while braiding her hair, she introduced Inner healing to me.

Inner healing is the key to changing negative self-images into positive ones. The only means of truly becoming all God has planned for the Believer, the freedom to reach the ultimate goal, comes through healing all stressful memories of yesterday from the womb to the last moment of time. The goal of inner healing is peace. It is about the healing of the broken, crushed emotional being. The dismissing or releasing of those shattered by the calamities of their yesterday's. Forgiveness releases the past hurts and stresses. The inner healing then heals the past in the total memory of the Believer. It does not blot out the memory of the believer, but it does discharge the stress. She asked me, do you have memories that cause pain?

"Yes, ma'am."

She reminded me that this pain could be rooted in past experiences as far as pre-birth memories and others as far back as my childhood, and the inner healing was something I needed. She then asked me, "If that was something I wanted to do, and even though I had never heard of inner healing before talking to her, I knew I could trust her, so I wanted to do it! I could tell her anything with such ease, and I know she took a lot to her grave! The next day was our first session. We walked into another room of her house, and she said, "I want you to close your eyes, and I'm going to begin to pray while playing some music."

I remember hearing those words so vividly play over and over in my head. My great-grandmother graciously glided across the floor in her walker and began the inner healing session with me. It intrigued me when she told me about its effects and how much it can help me.

And so, when we began this journey, I trusted her; I loved

her. I knew that what was about to happen was going to change my life. However, I was also nervous because I didn't know what was to come. I remember taking a deep breath and being at peace to allow whatever would happen to happen. I remember her saying I had to be willing to allow the Holy Spirit to move.

Inner healing is an extremely powerful and life-changing tool if used correctly and done with the Word of God. Inner healing has the power to change how you respond to trauma. In addition, inner healing can change how you deal with codependency relationships. I wanted my great-grandmother to show me what it meant to have complete inner healing. Unfortunately, I did not get that experience fully because she passed before we could get another session. But the one session that I had with her changed my life completely. I no longer feel the pain of those memories brought up in that first session. Of course, I remember them, but I no longer feel the pain associated with the memory. I will never forget our first and last inner healing session.

She told me that it was okay to be nervous, but there was nothing to be afraid of; she would be there with me, and I would feel so much better. I can still picture her antique furniture and how it was positioned in the room. We were sitting in two chairs facing each other, like in a counseling session. Still, the atmosphere was a lot warmer and more welcoming. She turned on some worship music. We sat in silence for a few minutes, and the tears just began to flow. I didn't know why, but I could feel that she was praying. And the entire dynamic of the room shifted. I could feel the presence of God resting on my shoulders. I could feel the anointing of my great-grandmother and the desire for inner healing within her family.

I felt so honored in this moment because if you ever had a chance to be in the presence of Apostle Rubye Durden, you know she was such a powerful, anointed woman. When you walked into her house, the atmosphere was so pure you couldn't help but feel safe and at peace. I can still smell her perfume. She almost always had company because everybody loved her. She always answers the phone. Jesus loves you! Which says a lot about her character in her heart for the people of God. She founded a ministry school and was a spiritual mother of several sons and daughters. Every time I was around her, she shifted my perspective on whatever we talked about that day. She always wanted me to braid her hair, and when I did, she always taught me something. She is truly my guardian angel.

She began to pray and asked me to repeat after her. "Father, in the name of Jesus, I ask you Holy Spirit to bring to my memory, conscious or subconscious, anyone I need to forgive in Jesus' name."

And as I began to repeat after her, a few negative memories from my parents and sisters came up. He began to show me faces of people I need to forgive. One particular memory involving my parents made me cry, and the tears just wouldn't stop. I needed to release all those negative emotions associated with the people and or memories still affecting me. I remember her humming the words to the song that was playing and praying in her prayer language. She just sat there and let me release it.

After I was done, she asked me how I felt. Then she said, "Now repeat after me, "Father in the name of Jesus by the act of my will, I choose to forgive _____ (insert name) I thank you,

Father, that I do forgive them and release them to you and receive my forgiveness from you."

She said, "Now I want you to do this for every person that God flashed in your mind. Take your time." I remember us continuing to do this for maybe an hour or so. Until she said, we could stop for the day and pick it back up another day. We prayed, and she dismissed us. I was exhausted, but I still felt light as a feather.

I went straight to my room and went to sleep because I was completely drained. The next day she gave me a few scriptures to read and meditate on and bought me the new Israel Houghton album. She said, "Always remember forgiveness is for you, not the other person. You will feel the effects of unforgiveness in your body. So, make sure you release and forgive immediately, even if you don't feel like it." Those words stuck with me. I will never forget the peace I experienced after this inner healing session with my great-grandmother. It was a burden lifted off me that I didn't know I needed to release, but I'm so glad I did. I wish I could've gotten more sessions and words of wisdom before she passed, but I'm grateful for the guide she left to our family and to the rest of the world for inner healing. I'm so excited to share this part of my great-grandmother with the rest of the world.

The next words and steps you will read come from the heart of my great grandmother to yours. I pray that these steps will guide you, and you will allow the Holy Spirit to give you peace that only He can provide.

In her book PEACE, she mentions the ministry (STEPS) OF INNER HEALING.

1. Listen

A. localize the problem,

B. Distinguish between surface and root problems.

C. After binding the enemy, ask Jesus to reveal specific conscious or subconscious memory patterns that he wishes healed.

2. Release the past.

A. Through forgiveness.

B. By leading in prayer, asking Lord Jesus to heal the memory and give his kind of forgetfulness of all related stress. (See suggested prayer and procedure.)

C. Have a friend pray with you. (Matthew 18: 19, "Again I say unto to you that if two of you shall agree on earth as touching anything that they shall ask, it shall be done for them of my Father which is in heaven.

D. Remember He suffered your wounds. (1 Peter 2:24) Who himself bore our sins and his own body on the tree, that we, being dead to sin, should live unto righteousness; by those stripes, you were healed.

Caution: To the close friend praying with the Believer;

1. Oral confession of the memory IS NOT NECESSARY unless the person feels it is necessary to share it. They may say, I have a memory. At that time, the healing prayer may be uttered. Remember, one's personal life IS personal.

2. Do not let the individual introspect.

3. Remember, this is the Lord's ministry wanna stay attuned to what he is doing.

4. Do not systemized or categorize the work of the Holy Spirit.

5. Undergird and develop the person's face as it often takes great strength and courage to face the reality of painful memories. Do not push.

SUGGESTED PRAYER AND PROCEDURE

Close friend (binding of the enemy)

Satan, all fallen angels, all unclean spirits, in the name of Jesus, you are bound and broken over _____ (name of the believer), myself, and this ministry. You cannot speak, act, work, hinder, go before, proceed after, keep from recall, cause recall, or input deceptive recall in Jesus's name.

CLOSE FRIEND (BINDING ENEMY)

The WORD states are foolish wars against our spirit. With your permission (get permission), I now rebuke your flesh and commanded to remain silent in this inner healing, in Jesus name. Father, your word states were to a more are gathered together in Jesus name, he is there we are gathered together in Jesus name, and I confess Jesus is here in this room to minister inner healing. He is the healer, the Baptizer, the Deliverer, Lord, Savior, and King of the Universe.

Nothing is done except He does it. Thank you, Jesus, for this ministry.

CLOSE FRIEND (TO BELIEVER)

Jesus will now show you the first memory or memories He wants healed. Only in severe cases will you find that the memory is too painful for them to acknowledge it; consequently, you will have to depend on your spiritual gifts to reveal the memory he wants healed and pray the prayer:

"Almighty Father, in the name of Jesus, by the power of the Holy Spirit, I lift this memory/memories to you for the healing, choosing never again to identify with the stress of it/them. Heal me of the memory/memories, And give me holy forgetfulness, your kind of forgetfulness, of all the stress/stresses. I confess I am healed in Jesus name.

(AFFIRMING PRAYER BY A CLOSE FRIEND)

Father, In Jesus name, I witness and attest that this/these memory /memories is/are healed in Jesus name; that forgetfulness is flowing and that the enemy cannot again program this/these memory/memories as they are healed now in Jesus name.

Note: This may continue until the believer is finished or until the Lord indicates by no more revealed memories the ministry is over for that session.

CLOSE FRIEND:

Father, I speak to the spirit of_____ (Believers name,) and say, spirit of_____ (Believers name)   You are healed from all wounding of this/these memory/memories in Jesus name.

Heart of _____(Believer's name) you are bound up of all broken-heartedness in Jesus name.

Will of_____(Believer's name) you are healed of your crushes in Jesus name. Now come forth with full authority in Jesus name.

CAUTION SHOULD BE USED in prolonging sessions of inner healing. This is a WHOLE MAN Ministry, and the person can often fatigue. It is never necessary to finish all of inner healing needs in one session. It is important as pacifically he'll pre-birth memories from the womb.

THERE'S ONLY ONE KIND OF INNER HEALING THAT IS WORD-BASED and that is the inner healing word Jesus is sovereign.

Walking back through the memories and seeing Jesus there is a form of my manipulation or auto suggestion. Using the imagination of power of the mind in any way is NOT WORD BASED.

Almighty God knows what memories need healing and can SOVEREIGNLY bring them forward in the believers mind or through the manifestations of the Holy Spirit in the Word of Wisdom or the Word of Knowledge.

DON'T TRY TO ASSIST GOD- HE IS BIG ENOUGH TO DO HIS MINISTRY HIS WAY.

"The Spirit of the Lord God is upon me; because the Lord has anointed me to preach good tidings until the meek; He had sent me to bind up the brokenhearted, to proclaim liberty to the captives, and the opening of the prison to them that are bound; to proclaim the acceptance year of the Lord, and the day of vengeance of our God; to comfort all that mourn. Isaiah 61:1-2

Sis, this check-in is different than the other ones, and this check-in should leave you with a peace that only the Holy Spirit can give. We must choose forgiveness daily, release bitterness and anger to fully embrace inner healing.

I know it's hard to forgive the person who abused, hurt, or mistreated you, but you MUST. You deserve to experience peace in your mind, body, and soul. Don't let anyone take your power from you. If you want to experience peace you must embrace this phase of forgiveness through Inner healing.

You Good Sis! You can do this!

YOU GOOD, SIS MENTAL HEALTH CHECK-IN (TAKE A 15–20-MINUTE BREAK)

1. Pause, and take a deep breath
2. You good, Sis? (Ask yourself, am I ok? Do I need a break?) If so, put the book down and come back to it.
3. What did this chapter bring up for you?
4. Were you triggered? If so, let's explore it. Grab your journal, your favorite pen, get your blanket

and let's write. Write what you felt; cry, release, and replace all negative beliefs with positive beliefs.

Chapter 10

Pain. Power. Purpose.

Whew, Sis! You made it! We made it to the end... I am so grateful to you for going through my journey with me. So many of the stories I wrote in this book were difficult to tell for so many reasons. To be honest, they were hard to acknowledge and live with. When I decided to be obedient and follow God's lead about what should and shouldn't be in this book, how and when to tell my story, it seemed like I started getting attacked from every direction. I suffered from anxiety and depression more than I ever had experienced before. I began to struggle with things that I thought I had conquered in my past. Although I was fasting and praying during the entire time of writing this book, it seemed as if the closer I got to God, the further the enemy tried to push me away. The more I began to share my truths and study God's word, the enemy started to attack my mind, my confidence to speak and share boldly with the same tactics he tried before. While writing this chapter, God revealed to me that I was experiencing the labor pains of birthing this baby; My baby, my gift to you. My heart, my pains, and of course, my triumphs.

I had to conquer the thoughts of feeling unworthy while battling imposter syndrome. It was not easy. I definitely couldn't have done it alone. I surrounded myself with people who could help me grow in the areas I was lacking. I have a therapist, of course, but I also sought out other professional support through coaching. My coaches are the best! They have helped me get to this point in my life. With the help of my Purpose Mindset Coach Kristie Lacy, I was able to shift my perspective and ultimately retrain my brain to operate in a consistent and intentional state. For years I always thought a lot of what I was dealing with or had been through was just because of my childhood experiences. But some things are our brain's natural response to situations. If someone said something negative about me or had a negative thought, I would immediately combat that thought with the truth. I affirm myself that it's okay for me to embrace the positive thoughts and stand boldly in my truth.

When I was a little girl, God showed me the call He had on my life, the lives that my story will touch, and the stages I would stand on. I was always so grateful for it all, but I also thought, what if this situation came out, or someone posted my mug shot. I wondered what people would think of me. So, I decided to take my power back and share my mistakes and weaknesses. I am human, and I will never be perfect. Even now, expressing my heart and all that I have learned, I know that my vulnerability could change a person's life. Those who have been in similar situations need to know they have support. I'm learning it's not just about writing your story but actually living out what you speak about it.

Information without implementation is just words on a paper.

I began to understand that transparency and relatability were the keys to helping as many women as I possibly can transform into the women that God has called them to be. I began to understand who I was, who I am, and who I am becoming. I studied and learned my personality type, the behavior traits that I carry, and what it would feel like to be a friend or be in a relationship with me. I begin to understand other people's perspectives. I recognized my vulnerability was my superpower. The more I began to speak about things that I had been through in my life, share my story with others, process through the pain with therapy, I was empowered more and began my lifelong healing journey. I learned my role in different situations and how I could affect a different outcome if the situation presented itself again. I understood that this was deeper than just me telling my story because everybody has a story. But it was about breaking generational curses, canceling demonic assignments off of our bloodlines which requires a lot of intentional work on the inside.

We start with forgiving and healing in our hearts first, then our families and bloodlines. We are raising up a generation that embodies talking about their emotions in healthy environments. Surrounding themselves with people that promote healthy boundaries. Educating our children on trauma, trauma bonds, and emotional intelligence. We must begin to communicate as healthy individuals and embrace what it means to live fully, love freely, and embrace the journeys ahead. We should embrace fear and rejection head-on and empower others who need it mentally and emotionally.

When you learn to speak from a healed place, you're not easily offended. My defense was always on 1000%. I never really responded to a situation; I just reacted. I now pause in the moment to reevaluate what the situation is. Is this something that I need to give my energy to? Do I need to sacrifice finances, resources, or my peace? And if I do, what does that look like, and how does that help me? Creating healthy boundaries can be terrifying when you are a people pleaser because you feel like if you stop making people happy, then it's a reflection of you as a person, or they may leave or reject you.

My identity was so wrapped into what other people thought of me. I often looked at the person I was in a relationship or friendship with to ask their viewpoint of how I was in situations. Usually, I would hear a different perspective, one I didn't agree with, but I moved and operated on what they said. I began to live out those things because of their position in my life or the standard I held them to. Now walking in my true identity and authority, this new power and boldness is refreshing but can be scary at times. It's a reminder that I am still growing and healing. I will get to the place where God wants me to be in my life. I believe in the woman that I am becoming. I visualize my highest, successful, and healed self and show up as her. I am limitless, and anything is possible. I try to be the best version of myself that I can, showing up even when it's hard and when I don't feel like it. Reminding myself this call on my life is greater than my emotions.

I pray that we would affirm the next generation of women to fully embody what self-care and self-love look and feels like. When we begin to look at this from the perspective of our daughters, granddaughters, and great-granddaughters, we ask ourselves what they need from us that the previous generations didn't provide; that's progress.

I fully embrace this self-awareness and self-discovery phase in my life. It's like seeing your life without trauma lenses. I lived most of my life behind trauma lenses, and I saw everything through a defensive lens. Recently I went to the movies with my daughters for our family day, and we went to see Black Widow. The movie showed how one man controlled the minds of young women who had been "thrown away" by society. They were a combination of women who were prostitutes, homeless, and abandoned by their families. He trained and conditioned them to kill, kidnap and destroy any and everything at his command. They were completely under his control, including his daughter.

At the end of the movie, Black Widow is fighting against about 20 widows, trying to survive and not hurt them because she knows they can't control their actions. Another widow came into the room and released an agent in the air. Within seconds, their mindsets shifted, and their behaviors changed. They stopped fighting and immediately began to help the widow. They didn't understand what had happened to them. They did know their behaviors and poor choices were largely due to what the villain had done to alter their minds.

I would love for the ending to be that they all went to get therapy, became healthy and whole individuals, and tried to give back to the other women who had been affected. But unfortunately, our society doesn't encourage and promote healing from emotional and mental trauma. Black Widow gave me a different perspective on trauma lenses and how we can allow them to influence our lives in positive and negative ways.

We sometimes use trauma lenses as crutches or excuses for behavior patterns we have. Sometimes we use them as excuses to hurt people who may or may not have hurt us. Remove the trauma lenses from your life. You good, Sis, I promise.

Start first with forgiving that parent, friend, or spouse. Let go of the toxic relationships in your life (family and friends included). Schedule a session with a therapist and/or life coach and surround yourself with people and friends who align with where you are in your life right now and where you want to be.

Support during this journey is so important when you are on your road to healing. Let's heal together, Sis. Process through your trauma and release anything that doesn't serve you in this season of your life. I love you, Sis; I am here for you, and I am proud of you for embarking on this journey.

Let's get to this inner healing work together and bring all the women we know around us. We have the power to shift the next generation and the things they will have to go through. Some of our parents are still dealing with certain battles but don't understand why their child/children are repeating the same things. We can't empower our children to change if we won't lead by example.

You good, Sis Mental Health Check-in (Take a 15–20-minute break)

1. Pause, and take a deep breath
2. You good, Sis? (Ask yourself, am I ok? Do I need a break?) If so, put the book down and come back to it.

3. What did this chapter bring up for you?

4. Were you triggered? If so, let's explore it. Grab your journal, your favorite pen, get your blanket and let's write. Write what you felt; cry, release, and replace all negative beliefs with positive beliefs.

References

Complex PTSD: From Surviving to thriving, Pete Walker

More Than Anything. (song) Anita Wilson

Peace by Rubye Durden

Jeremy Foster Sermon Series -Rhythms

What is Rejection Sensitivity?
https://www.verywellmind.com

5 Ways Mentally Strong People Deal With Rejection |
Inc.com. https://www.inc.com/

Acknowledgments

"You Good, Sis?" wouldn't be possible without the amazing people who have supported me on this journey. I am forever grateful to my amazing parents Ross Cullins Jr and Shonda Cullins, for loving and supporting me in my journey to help other women through my story. Thank you for teaching me the word of God, giving me the tools to navigate through this journey of life. Thank you for allowing me to be transparent so that others will be healed. I love you so much and am so glad God chose you as my parents. I would not be who I am today without your constant prayers, support, and encouragement.

To my four beautiful daughters Camille, Cayleigh, Chloe, & Aundrea: Thank you for your sacrifice, patience, and support while writing this book. Mommy is so proud of each one of you, and I love you so much. I pray you read this book and are empowered to share your experiences with the world too. You are the legacy I leave this book to.

To the father of my children, Joshua Colquitt, my friend, confidant, and co-partner in raising our girls. Thank you for your unwavering support throughout all the years of my life. You have supported me consistently since 11th grade in high school, good or bad. I appreciate all of your sacrifices and encouragement when I didn't want to live life anymore. You were there when nobody else was, and I'm forever grateful for you.

To my six beautiful sisters: Kivante, Geohnita, Crystal, Ashley, Gabrielle, and Eva: I appreciate your support, encouragement, and motivation to keep going when I wanted to stop writing because it was overwhelming at times. Thank you for reminding me this will help somebody, and I had no choice but to keep going! Thank you for being my rock, my support team, and always my cheerleaders.

To my Great-mother Rubye Durden, whose life experiences and book entitled Peace helped build the foundation for this book. I pray her words of wisdom, anointed prayers, and inner healing guide shall penetrate the hearts of all those who will read this book, and I am honored to have been in her presence and get to know her. As a child, watching her lead her ministry, Soul Spiration, train women in her ministry school, and still, hear so many amazing things about her even after her death confirms that I am aligned with the legacy she created. I pray you are pleased with my efforts to continue it.

To my Granny Linda Cullins, I love you! Thank you for always supporting me, praying for me, and correcting me when I am wrong. Thank you for creating the first safe place for me as a child to be vulnerable and share my pains without judgment. I am forever grateful to know you never judged me, but you allow me to be me. You encouraged me to grow in ways spiritually I didn't know I needed to. Watching you deal with mental illnesses and overcome them is so inspiring to me. I'm so honored to be your "favorite" firstborn grandchild and the bond we share.

To my favorite PAWPAW, my one, and only grandfather. Thank you for leading our family by the example you live through your life daily. You have always shown me I don't have to settle in relationships. You are the example I look to when I consider what type of man I want in life. You instilled in all of us at a very young age the importance of studying scripture and living out the word daily. Thank you for the long conversations about any and everything. I cherish the value, wisdom, and compassion you have always shown me and continue to show throughout my life. Your presence is my life and has been my motivation and encouragement to live out my God-given purpose. Thank you for paving the way for us to serve freely in ministry.

To my Grandy, Dandy Levy-Cullins, my first example of how a First Lady should carry herself. I desired to be one just like you one day because you made it look so easy. You are the epitome of a Proverbs 31 woman. You sacrificed so much for us throughout the years and never expected anything in return. You always made sure you taught us what the word said about certain things. Morning devotionals with you and pawpaw taught me the importance of it. They encouraged me to pass it on to my children. You have had a huge impact on my life, and I am grateful for your love, support, and consistent prayers and leadership. When I called you to get your thoughts when I started writing the book, you were so proud, and your feedback had a huge impact on what I put in the book. Thank you!

To my best friends Antoinette Reve-McLane, Cora Jakes-Coleman, Tashawna Mathew's, and Ciara Smith, who understood the magnitude of what writing this book entailed and prayed for me, fasted with me and motivated me. Each of you was with me through the bulk of the roller coasters in my life. You are still standing strong with me, and I am forever grateful. Thank you for your contributions, late-night talks, and sometimes just making sure I knew you were there to support me. I am grateful to have your friendships, prayers, and accountability.

To my support system: My coaches, Book Coach Tara Tucker, Business Coach-Maelan Taylor, Purpose Mindset Coach Kristie Lacy, and my Speaking Coach Destiny Inspire. Each one of you has challenged me and pushed me into my purpose. I couldn't have done this without your consistent accountability, encouragement, and support to show up as my best self-daily. Watching you show up for me and your clients inspired me to do the same. Your vulnerabilities, life experiences, and testimonies you shared to show me you were relatable were powerful enough for me to walk in my superpower. Thank you for your individual roles in my life. Thank you for always adding value to my life. I am forever grateful to you.

Last but certainly not least, I want to thank each and every one of you for your support in my movement. For every person who came into the *You Good Sis. Mental Health Check in* on Clubhouse every week and supported my journey, thank you! To every person that purchased lipsticks or simply shared my post on social media, thank you! To everyone who purchased this book and even bought one for other people, thank you.

I love you and appreciate you,

Your Sis, your Battle Buddy Monet 🖤🖤

About the Author

Monet Cullins is the CEO of Bold Lips Revolution Cosmetics, a Transformational Speaker, and the founder of The Battle Buddies Tribe, a nonprofit women empowerment platform specializing in helping women push past their battles in mental health and domestic violence  through safety planning, support, and resources.

Monet's desire to see women grow and revolutionize their self-image was birthed from the 7 years she was a victim of domestic violence and overcoming childhood trauma. After struggling with low self-esteem for many years of her adolescence & adult life, she wanted to make a difference in the lives of young women. Monet wanted to find a way to encourage women to find confidence after abuse and embrace their true identity. After escaping her abusive relationship, she started a cosmetics line while living in a domestic violence shelter to give back and help other victims. She helps women rediscover their power through her beauty emPOWERment brand. Her cosmetics line donates a portion of the proceeds to survivors of domestic violence.

Monet and her remarkable journey from Victim to Victory have been featured twice on WFAA News 8 at Daybreak #iamstillup in Dallas, Good Morning Texas, and the social media pages of KPRC Click 2 Houston & KHOU 11 News Houston, and several other news media outlets. Monet has done motivational speaking at church conferences, community functions, empowerment calls, and even live from her own social media pages with her inspiring story and passion for people. Monet aspires to continue to use her message of survival as stretched arms to hug every woman who finds themselves in a position of self-doubt worldwide. She is a mom of four beautiful daughters Camille, Cayleigh, Chloe, & Aundrea.

website : www.blrcosmetics.com

Battle Buddies Tribe

The Battle Buddies Tribe is a 501C3 women empowerment platform specializing in helping women push past their domestic violence battles, mental health through emergency support services, and a new foundation to begin their healing journey.

We provide a safe and secure environment for women who have suffered abuse, create a safety plan that is protected by "buddy words." We provide counseling resources and ultimately a sisterhood of support.

The Battle Buddies Tribe was birthed from a brunch in 2019, with the hopes of creating sisterhood and a safe place for when they need it the most. When I was in the shelter, they required me to complete a safety plan if something happened. Well, I wasn't comfortable putting my family and friends down that knew him. It didn't make sense to create a safety plan with people still connected with your abuser. So, I created a 3-part buddy system, Favorite Buddy, Support Buddy, and Comfort Buddy. These buddies are trained to assess your situation, and with the use of the code word established between you and your support buddy, get you to safety.

FAVORITE BUDDIES are Police Officers, Lawyers, Nurses, & Shelters. Your favorite buddy is someone you reach out to when you are in a life-threatening emergency. If you are in a situation and need immediate assistance, this is the option for you. This option is like pulling the alarm; if you are in a life-threatening emergency, we're coming for you!

COMFORT BUDDIES are licensed professionals and or counselors who can reach out for emotional support, mental health checks, and advice. They will be there to talk through whatever it is that you need. If you find yourself needing clarity and peace of mind, this is the option for you. We will connect you with the best person to meet your needs.

SUPPORT BUDDIES is a fellow Battle Buddy trained to help support you and has experienced similar circumstances. They are here to stand alongside you as you travel this new journey together. So, if you just need a listening ear and a no-judgment zone. This option is for you!

Visit me on CLUBHOUSE:

Join OUR CLUB 💜 The Battle Buddies Tribe 💜

Come join our room

"You good, Sis?" Mental Health Check-In MWF 11:30 CST

BOOK ME for Speaking Engagements

Info@yougoodsis.club

If you know someone who has experienced domestic violence & they need support.

📱 Text BUDDY to 814-808-5321

Join our FREE Facebook Support Group: The Battle Buddies Tribe

Let's Connect: hello@wearebattlebuddiestribe.org

For more information visit

www.wearebattlebuddiestribe.org

CPSIA information can be obtained
at www.ICGtesting.com
Printed in the USA
FSHW010503011221
86516FS